WordPerfe

for Windows

C000319865

PRISMA Computer Courses are structured, practical guides to mastering the most popular computer programs. PRISMA books are course books, giving step-by-step instructions, which take the user through basic skills to advanced functions in easy to follow, manageable stages.

Now available:

Excel 4.0 for Windows
Lotus 1-2-3 2.4
MS-DOS 3.3 to 5.0
Windows 3.0 and 3.1
WordPerfect 5.1
WordPerfect for Windows

WordPerfect for Windows

PRISMA COMPUTER COURSE

PRISMA Computer Coursesfirst published in Great britain 1992 by

McCarta Ltd
P.O. Box 2996
N5 2TA London

Translation: George Hall
Production: LINE UP text productions
© 1993 Uitgeverij Het Spectrum B.V., Utrecht

ISBN 1 85365 370 5

British Libary Cataloguing-in-Publication Data.
A catalogue record for this book is available from the British Libary.

Contents

Appendices

Foreword

This book is primarily for those who wish to learn quickly
how to work with WordPerfect for Windows. A 1220-
page manual is supplied along with the program, but it
is really not necessary to read all this in order to be able
to work with the program. In this book, the basic word
processing functions and layout will be dealt with, along
with a number of special features. The new possibilities
with respect to the DOS versions of WordPerfect will be
discussed with particular emphasis on the layout possibilities which begin to resemble the more specialised
DTP (Desktop Publishing) programs.

Other programs which the WordPerfect user may encounter are also discussed. Descriptions and explana-
tions are supported by practical examples and exercises.
Anyone who wishes to fully understand WordPerfect for
Windows is advised to try out the features which are dealt
with in this book and to carry out the exercises.

For PC users who have no prior knowledge of Windows, the appendices C and D instruct you how to install Windows 3.1 and how to work with this program. In
addition, general software information and computer
terminology can be found in appendices E and F. Regardless of what you decide to read or to skip, take the
time to approach the first chapter with an open mind. It
may open the window to an interesting world.

1   Introduction

In a relatively short time, the WordPerfect word processing program developed into the most commonly used program in the whole world. In the United States, Canada and in various European countries including Great Britain, WordPerfect is the best-selling and most-used program for word processing on the PC. The fact that special versions for the East European languages are being brought onto the market (Russian and Czech versions were already available in 1991) is an indication that WordPerfect will maintain its leading position internationally.

An attractive feature of WordPerfect is that personal use is stimulated. In fact, an official statement was made in 1991 that business users who work with WordPerfect in the office may copy the program in order to work with it at home, as long as it is not used on more than one computer simultaneously.

Since the introduction of Windows 3.0 by Microsoft in 1990, this graphic MS-DOS 'user shell' has become enormously popular. An ever-increasing number of software manufacturers began to produce programs specifically for Windows. The benefits of Windows are evident - in word processing and DTP applications the user can see the result of each adjustment directly and immediately on the screen. Windows also provides other advantages - for instance, the method of working is identical for every program because the manufacturers have a strict agreement concerning the menus and function keys, and there is also the facility to work with different applications at one time.

Windows does have its drawbacks. The graphic presentation means that the software is more extensive and occupies more internal memory than programs which are started directly from MS-DOS (or DS-DOS). Although WordPerfect 5.1 is a heavyweight program under DOS, it can still be run on a PC/XT with 640 Kb

internal memory. Much more is required to run Word-
Perfect under Windows, since Windows already occupies so much memory. The windows version of
WordPerfect, referred to as WPWin by both the manufacturers and the author of this book, can only be run on
a PC/AT with a 80286 or more advanced processor with
a *minimum* of 2 Mb internal memory (RAM). Although
you will observe that WPWin does run on this minimum
configuration, you will also see that you will regularly
have to wait when using all kinds of functions. The only
real solution to this problem is to extend the RAM to 4
Mb. We shall discuss this further later on in this chapter.

A great advantage of WPWin is that files which are created using this program are interchangeable with files
created using LetterPerfect and WordPerfect 5.1 under
DOS. (The former program is a less extensive version
of WordPerfect, considerably cheaper and can be readily used on XTs with only 512 Kb memory and on computers without a harddisk.) Anyone who uses WPWin
on a fast computer at his/her work can further edit the
created files on an XT at home (or on a portable PC)
using WordPerfect 5.1 for DOS or LetterPerfect. And
anyone who has created a text file at home can quickly
rearrange the layout to suit his/her wishes using WPWin
and print it on a good printer without this process con-
suming too much time.

1.1   The layout of this book

Those who have not yet installed Windows 3.0 or 3.1
are advised to refer to appendix C, *Installing Windows*.
Those who have installed Windows but have not yet
worked with it to any great extent should devote some
study to appendix D, *Working with Windows*, but more
can be learned from a book specially aimed at this subject such as the Prisma Computer Course for Windows
3.0 and 3.1.

The demands on the system by Windows in general
and WPWin in particular are dealt with in appendix B.

Chapter 2 discusses the installation of WordPerfect for Windows and starting up and ending the program.

Chapter 3 deals with the actual word processing, chapter 4 with Help features such as hyphenation, spelling check and the list of synonyms. The possibility of having your style and grammar checked by help programs is also discussed. In chapter 5, there is a review of special functions which concern the screen display, or which help you to work more quickly and easily such as macros and the useful new *Button Bar*.

Chapter 6 discusses lettertypes or fonts and gives instructions not only about their settings but also about the choice of a particular font. Other matters which deal with the layout of a text, such as line spacing and the page layout are to be found in chapter 7. Here, you can also become acquainted with the Ruler, which is again a new feature of WPWin. Chapter 8 deals with images and lines and chapter 9 with DTP. Here you will find an outline of what this is exactly and how to work with it.

In chapter 10, you can become familiar with the File Manager program which is separately supplied along with WPWin. Subsequently, a number of special functions are dealt with - tables, combination, relocation. Chapters 12 and 13 provide examples of what is possible in practice using WPWin. Chapter 14 indicates what you should know about printing from WPWin and chapter 15 discusses extra possibilities.

The topic of macros is so extensive that WordPerfect has published a separate book about this, which is mainly directed at advanced users. In this book, the creation of macros is discussed but the information is presented in such a way that the average user will easily be able to handle the topic.

The appendices contain, in addition to general information about Windows, a Software Indicator. This is a survey of programs which cooperate with WPWin in one way or another or which allow you to get more out of your printer than the standard possibilities.

In addition, you will find in the appendices a list of common computer terminology and specific Windows and WordPerfect terminology.

1.2   Symbols and abbreviations

The computer function keys are referred to as F1, F2 etc. Other special keys are referred to as Tab, Shift etc. Moving the cursor is called Cursor Up, Cursor Down etc.

WordPerfect is also abbreviated to WP and WordPerfect for Windows to WPWin.

When installing WPWin, you may choose between two keyboard layouts. One is called the CUA keyboard, because the use of the function keys and suchlike conforms to the definitions of the Common User Access from Windows programs. Only if you choose this definition will the function keys and other specific key combinations work exactly as in other Windows programs. The other layout is aimed at users who are used to working with WordPerfect 5.0 or 5.1 for DOS but who are not (yet) planning to switch completely to Windows applications. In this case, the working of the function keys and suchlike deviates from that which is defined in Windows, but this does conform to a large extent to that for WordPerfect 5.1 for DOS.

Some functions can only be easily executed using a mouse. Almost any common computer mouse can be applied.

When working with certain functions is being described, the following symbols are used:

M   The text with this symbol outlines how to carry out the function making use of the mouse *as much as possible*. In many cases, this is the quickest work method.

K   The text with this symbol indicates how to execute the function *without* using the mouse, thus making *exclusive* use of the keyboard. Although this is sometimes faster, often it is less handy.

D   If you selected the keyboard layout which corresponds to WP DOS 5.1 during the installation of WPWin (see chapter 2), the text next to this symbol outlines how to execute the function using the keyboard. This is only indicated when the significance of function keys and/or key combinations differ from the usage in the previous symbol.

1.3   The exercises

For those who wish to practise immediately, there are exercises at the conclusion of most chapters. Each exercise can be carried out in different ways. Examples of the procedures are given under the exercises. In this, the quickest method is chosen as much as possible, in other words, the mouse and keyboard are used in combination in order to choose the required functions.

2   Installation and activation of WordPerfect for Windows

2.1   Before you begin

If you are going to install WordPerfect for Windows, Windows should already be installed. If that is not the case, first install Windows. See also *Installing Windows* (appendix C).

Before installing WordPerfect, it is advisable to make backup copies of the diskettes. Ensure that the original diskettes are write-protected, make the copies, store the original diskettes in a safe place and use the copies to install WPWin. Ensure that there are no unnecessary programs in memory before you begin.

2.2   Installing WordPerfect for Windows

Place the Installation/Program 1 diskette in diskdrive A: or B: (depending on the format) and activate the appropriate drive by typing **a:** (or **b:**) and pressing Enter. Now type:

```
install
```

and press Enter.

The opening screen *WordPerfect for Windows Installation* will appear with the question 'Would you like to continue?'
Type **y** (yes).

A list containing WordPerfect installation options will be shown.

```
WordPerfect Installation Options                 Installation Problems?
                                                   Contact WordPerfect

▶ 1 - Basic      Install standard files into default directories, for example
                 c:\wpwin\ and c:\wpc\).

  2 - Custom     Install standard files to directories you specify.

  3 - Network    Install standard files to a network drive.  Only a network
                 supervisor should use this option.

  4 - Printer    Install additional or updated WordPerfect Printer Files.

  5 - Interim    Install Interim Release program files.  Use this option only if
                 you are replacing existing WordPerfect for Windows files.

  6 - Copy       Install every file on a diskette into a directory you specify
                 (useful for installing all the Printer .ALL files).

  7 - Language   Install additional WordPerfect language modules.

  8 - README     View WordPerfect for Windows README files.


Selection: 1                                      (F1 for Help; Esc to exit)
```

You may choose from 8 possibilities or discontinue the installation by pressing the Esc key. As you will observe, F1 is used as the Help key. By pressing F1, you will receive information concerning the installation options.

In order to make a new installation of WPWin, you may choose from options 1, 2 and 3. If you choose 1, this will result in a standard installation in which WPWin will be placed in a new directory C:\WPWin and the supplementary programs will be placed in C:\WPC. More than 9 Mb disk capacity will be occupied. If you wish to install WPWin in another directory or on another drive, then you should choose option 2 - *Custom*. This provides, at the same time, the possibility of deciding whether certain supplementary programs should be placed on the disk. If there is not much space available, it is better not to install all programs.

We shall presume that you select option 2 by typing 2 or C. *Customised Installation* will appear on the screen. First check option 1 to see if the required diskdrive is shown. If this is not the case, type a 1. Then, at the bottom of the screen, you will be able to enter the appropriate drive. Type a 2 to specify where the files should be installed. The *Location of Files* screen will appear. By then typing a 1, you can specify where the WordPerfect for Windows program should be located.

That can be C:\WPWIN or D:\WPWIN (if you have several harddisks), or for instance a directory C:\PRO-GRAM.

When you have entered the required directory name, you will see a message (unless you have already made a directory beforehand):

```
Directory c:\wpwin\ does not exist.  Create
it?  Yes (No)
```

Type a **y** if the directory should be created, type an **n** if you have made a mistake and wish to specify a directory name once again.

WordPerfect automatically creates subdirectories of the specified directory. At the same time, a directory is made for shared products for this and future Windows programs from the WordPerfect Corporation. This prevents the same file being saved on disk twice or more, if, for example, you are going to use PlanPerfect or DrawPerfect for Windows. Unless you really wish to have a different installation, it is advisable to accept the proposed names. You do have to specify the directory in which you wish to place the documents which you make using WPWin, for instance, C:\TEXT or C:\LET-TERS or C:\WPDOC. Type a 2, and then enter the required directory at the bottom of the screen. If this does not yet exist, WordPerfect will ask if it should be created. When you have completed this procedure, type a 9 to return to the previous menu.

Option 3 is already marked - Perform Installation. Type a 3 or an I or press Enter to start up the installation.

```
WordPerfect File Installation


                    Available Disk Space
                            Drive:            F:
              Total Bytes on drive:    83,671,040
                       Bytes used:    64,473,088
                       Bytes free:    19,197,952
       Bytes required for all of WPWIN:     9,750,000
       Bytes free after full install:     9,447,952

       Do you wish to continue?  Yes (No)
```

You will see a survey of the available disk space. If there is too little space to install the program, you can now stop and consider whether other files on the disk may be deleted. Also keep in mind that WPWin does not occupy 9.75 Mb if you do not install certain parts and the companion programs. Nevertheless, it is much more convenient to install everything in one go. If you wish to proceed, type a **y** (yes).

Answer the question 'Do you want to install the Word-Perfect program?' by pressing Y. In the course of the installation, you will be asked if you wish to install various utility files. At the same time, a short outline is given concerning the function of these files. At the bottom of the screen, the programs which are placed in the speci-fied directories are shown. The installation program also creates a new WordPerfect group in Windows simulta-neously.

Follow the instructions given on the screen, switching disk-ettes when requested. Here is a concise survey of most of the questions you will be asked during the installation:

'Do you want to install the WordPerfect Help File?'. This deals with Help information which you can receive by pressing F1 when working with WordPerfect under Windows. Unless you are convinced that you will never use this function, answer Yes here.

'Do you want to install the WordPerfect Macros Help File?'. This only needs to be done if you are going to write you own macros.

The following question will appear - 'Do you want to install the Button Bar, Keyboard and Macro Files?'. The button bar is an extremely useful tool in WPWin. We advise you to answer Yes.

Then there is the question 'Do you want to install the Macro Conversion Program?'. This concerns the program which can convert macros created in the DOS version of WordPerfect to macros which can be applied in the Windows version. If this is not needed, answer No.

The question 'Do you want to install the Style Library?' should receive the answer Yes if you wish to work through this book effectively. However, the Style Library is not essential for working with WPWin.

'Do you want to install WordPerfect Button Bar Picture Files?'. We advise you to answer Yes.

In a separate window in the lower half of the screen, the question is raised concerning the installation of files for the monitor display. You may allow files to be installed which regulate various monitors, but if you are not planning to replace the screen or video card, it is advisable to only install the file which runs the monitor now in use. Thus, a negative answer here saves roughly 600 Kb disk capacity.

'Do you want to install the Learning/Workbook Files?'. This only needs to be done if you are going to work through the lessons in the WordPerfect exercise book. Not installing these files saves disk capacity.

'Do you want to install the Graphics Files?'. This concerns graphics files with the extension .WPG (WordPerfect Graphics) which you can use to illustrate your documents. They are also used in the examples in this book. Unless you are not planning to use pictures at all, answer Yes here.

The question 'Do you want to install the Shared Product Files?' appears on the screen. This concerns files which will be used for all WordPerfect Windows programs - File Manager, Speller, printer drivers etc. If you have not yet installed any other WordPerfect Windows products (such as PlanPerfect or DrawPerfect in a special Windows version), you should respond with Y(es). Switch diskettes when necessary and press a random key, for example Enter or the spacebar, but not Esc since this would lead to a part of the installation process being skipped.

Subsequently, the question 'Do you want to install the Macro Facility?' appears on the screen. This deals with a file which is needed to create and run macros in WPWin. If you are not planning to use this, you may answer No, but remember that macros can lighten your workload considerably.

The next question is 'Do you want to install the Macro Command Inserter?'. If you are not planning to use this, you may answer No.

The next question is 'Do you want to install the File Manager?' The File Manager is a companion program which enables you to copy, delete and move files, create and delete directories etc. (If you are familiar with the DOS version of WP 5.1, you will know that this function is implemented by pressing F5. In the Windows version this has become a separate program with new possibilities.) If you think that you will not need the WordPerfect program for File Manager, since you already manage your files in another way, answer No to save diskspace. If you do wish to use the File Manager from WP, respond Yes and the program will be installed.

When working with Windows programs, you can always request extra information by pressing the Help key (F1). This also applies to WPWin and to companion programs which you can install such as Speller, Thesaurus and WordPerfect File Manager. The next question is 'Do you want to install the Shared Product Help Files?'. Keep in mind, before answering, that this merely concerns programs which can be separately used, Speller, Thesaurus and File Manager, and not the WPWin program itself.

The next question is 'Do you want to install Utility Files?'. These are programs for converting graphic files, for extending the exceptions list in the hyphenation process and for self-editing of the Speller word lists. Probably only advanced users will have need of these programs.

Then you will be asked if you wish to install the Printer program. This is a file dealing with adjustment to the printer driving (for which specialized know-how is required) and for automatic font replacement. The latter provides a good reason for installing the program if you are working with different printers.

'Do you want to install the Speller?'. This deals with a separate program which can be activated from WPWin in order to check the spelling in the document you have made.

'Do you want to install the Thesaurus?'. This is a list of synonyms and antonyms which can be activated in WPWin. We shall deal with this program later.

2.3   The keyboard definition

Now comes an important question - which keyboard definition do you wish to use? To be perfectly clear - this does *not* concern which keyboard is attached to your computer. That question has already been answered during the Windows installation.

You can always use the keys a to z and 1 to 0 to type letters and numbers. What we are dealing with here is the way in which you wish to use the function keys F1 to F12 and the key combinations with Alt and Ctrl.

■ If you are going to use Windows program (almost) exclusively in the future, choose CUA, *Common User Access.* This means that, for **all** Windows programs including WPWin, these keys (key combinations) have the following significance: F1 for Help, F4 for opening files, Alt-F4 for ending the program, F5 for printing, F8 for selecting, F9 for choosing the font etc.

■ If you are already accustomed to working with Word-Perfect under DOS and you are *not* going to use other Windows programs or are planning to also keep on using the DOS version of WP, it may be useful to select the other possibility, the WordPerfect for DOS keyboard.

In that case, the following keys (key combinations) have significance: F1 (still) for Help, Shift-F10 for opening files, F7 for ending, Shift-F7 for printing, Alt-F4 for selecting, Ctrl-F8 for selecting a font etc.

Type 1 if you wish to use the keyboard in accordance with the CUA version, or 2 if you wish to use the (more or less) WP 5.1 for DOS keyboard. You can, if required, alter this definition later.

You will now return to the *Customised Installation* menu. The program is installed, only the printers remain to be chosen. If WordPerfect 5.1 for DOS is already on disk, you can use the same printer driver. Then you have to select the printer(s) later from WPWin and specify the directory in which the printer files are located.
If you have to install a new printer, is makes sense to select it while the installation program is running, since the consequent saving of disk capacity is minimal if you were to opt for the printer driver already installed.

2.4   Installing printers

When you have opted for Select Printer(s), you will be asked, just to be sure, whether you wish to make use of the WordPerfect printer driver programs. If you assign the operation of the printer driver to Windows, then you have rid yourself of the problem, but this does have its drawbacks. We shall return to this in chapter 7 of this book.

```
▶  A - AGFA Compugraphic 9400PS
   B - Apple LaserWriter                        Printer Driver Selection
   C - Apple LaserWriter IIg
   D - Apple LaserWriter IINT           Use the arrow keys, PgUp, and
   E - Apple LaserWriter IINTX          PgDn to move the pointer (▶)
   F - Apple LaserWriter Plus           through the printer list.
   G - ASCII Text Printer               Then press Enter to install a
   H - Blaser Star 2                    printer driver.
   I - Brother 2024L
   J - Brother HJ-100                   After a printer driver is
   K - Brother HJ-770                   installed it is marked with a
   L - Brother HL-4                     diamond (◆).
   M - Brother HL-4PS
   N - Brother HL-4V                    If your printer is not shown
   O - Brother HL-8D                    on the list, press F1 for more
   P - Brother HL-8e                    information.
   Q - Brother HL-8PS
   R - Brother HL-8PS (HP)              A printer marked with an
   S - Brother HL-8V                    asterisk (✕) is not available
   T - Brother M-1109                   on these diskettes.  Select
   U - Brother M-1309                   option for more information.
   V - Brother M-1324

   F2 Name Search; PgDn More Printers; PgUp Previous Screen; F1 Help; Esc Cancel;
   Selection: A
```

If you answer Yes to this question, you should place *Printer 1* diskette in the appropriate drive. Press any key and a list of printer names will appear on the screen. If your printer sort and type is not displayed in the alphabetical list, press PageDown (NumLock must be off) until you find it. Then type the letter which is located in front of the printer name. You will be asked if you wish to select this printer - this is to prevent an unintentional selection. When this printer has been installed, another question will appear: 'Would you like to install another printer?'. If you respond Yes, *in addition to the selected printer* another printer will be installed.

Accordingly, you are able to work with different printers. If you wish, you can install more printers. If you answer

No, the installation provides the option of reading the Readme files. These contain supplementary information which has not yet been documented in the thick WordPerfect manual. However, it is not really beneficial to read this at this stage.

The next option is *README*. If you select this you will be presented with the contents of the README file of your choice (Wordperfect Program, Shared Program or Graphics/Learning).

You have now reached the option *Exit Installation*. You select this by typing a **6** or an **X**. You will then return to the DOS prompt. Type **C:** to choose the harddisk. Now you can start up WPWin via Windows.

2.5 Starting up WordPerfect for Windows

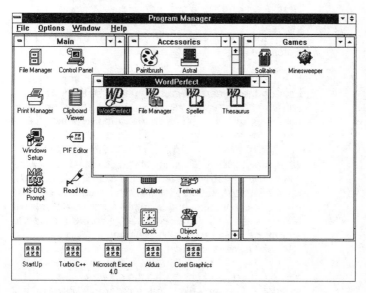

The first time you start up WordPerfect for Windows after the installation, the window of the new group Word-Perfect is located on top of the other windows (see picture on previous page).

As you see, the group now contains four programs:

■ WordPerfect: the word processing program;
■ File Manager: this is a program supplied along with WordPerfect which deals with moving, renaming, copying and deleting files and groups of files. This program is handier than the File Manager in the Windows Program Manager main group;
■ Speller: this is a program which can be used separately, but you will probably activate it mostly from WordPerfect;
■ Thesaurus: as in Speller.

WordPerfect can be activated by:

m   Double clicking the WordPerfect icon.

k   Since the WordPerfect icon is already marked, press Enter.

If you are doing this for the very first time, a frame will appear on the screen in which you must state the registration number of your WPWin package. The registration number is shown on a card in the wrapping of the original WPWin diskettes. If you have acquired the package as an upgrade of a DOS version, you will find this number in the wrapping of this DOS version. If you do not have the original number readily available, you can fill in a random number consisting of the letters **WP**, the country code **44** for the British version and six other numbers. In order to request help from WordPerfect UK, you are required to specify the proper registration number.
Click on OK or press Enter.

You must wait a moment until the printers specified during installation are linked to the program. Then you will see an almost empty screen.

At the very top of the screen there is the title bar containing the name of the program (WordPerfect) and the statement [Document1 - unmodified].

As soon as you type one letter, the statement 'unmodified' disappears. *Document1* remains as interim title until you save the text.

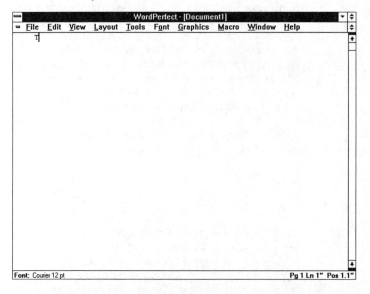

The Control menu button is located at the left of the title bar and the Minimize button and the Restore buttons at the right. (If you are not familiar with these terms, consult appendix D, *Working with Windows*.)

Inside the WordPerfect window, there is a window which is almost just as large. This is the document window, with the system menu button in the upper left-hand corner, a menu bar extending over the width of the screen and a Restore button in the top right-hand corner.

If you wish to make a selection from the menu, the following possibilities are available:

m   Click on one of the words in the menu bar. A drop-down
        menu will appear. Click on the required option. In cer-
        tain cases, a new drop-down menu will appear, or a dia-
        logue box.
        Again select the required option.

k   Simultaneously press the Alt key and the underlined let-
        ter in the menu: Alt-F for File, Alt-E for Edit etc. A drop-
        down menu will appear. Using Cursor Down, you can
        select an option and press Enter to confirm it, or you
        can type the underlined letter in the selected option.
        Sometimes another drop-down menu will appear and
        often a dialogue box. Only press Enter again when you
        have completely filled in the dialogue box.

        If you have activated a menu but do not (yet) wish to
        make a selection,

m   Click on a random place outside the drop-down menu.

k   Press Alt once again.

        Many menu options can be activated more quickly by
        using keystrokes, for instance F1 for Help, Alt-F1 for the
        Thesaurus, Alt-F8 for styles etc. Which key combination
        applies to which function depends to some extent on
        the keyboard definition chosen during installation.

        The font currently in use is displayed in the lower left-
        hand corner, and in the lower right-hand corner the cur-
        rent position of the cursor (the blinking black stripe) is
        registered. The scroll bar is displayed down the right-
        hand side. If the text does not entirely fit into the screen,
        you can display other parts of the text by clicking on the
        small arrows at the top and bottom of the scroll bar or by
        dragging the grey block using the mouse.

2.6   Ending WordPerfect

Ending WordPerfect is simple:

𝓜   Click on *File* in the menu bar and then on *Exit*. Alternatively, click on the WordPerfect control menu button (upper left corner) and on *Close*.

𝓚   Press Alt-F, then C. Alt-F4 (or Ctrl-F4) is quicker.

𝓓   Press Alt-F. F7 is quicker.

A dialogue box will appear on the screen: 'Save changes to Document1?' (or the name of the document if this has been allocated). The possibilities are as follows:

𝓜   Click on *Yes* to save the document in its current form. Click on *No* if you do not wish to save it. Click on *Cancel* if you wish to continue editing.

𝓚   Type Y if you wish to save the document in its current form. Type N if you do not wish to save it. Press Enter or Esc if you wish to edit it further.

2.7   Starting up WordPerfect again

Perhaps you have been working with another Windows program in the meantime and you wish to activate WordPerfect once more,

𝓜   Click on *Window* in the Program Manager menu, then click on *WordPerfect*. Then double click on the Word-Perfect icon.

𝓚   Press Alt-W. Type the number in front of 'WordPerfect'. If the WordPerfect icon is not yet highlighted, press Cursor Left until that is the case. Then press Enter.

Actual word processing will be discussed in the following chapter.

3   Typing and editing text

3.1   Beginning a document

Each piece of text made using WordPerfect and saved
as a separate file is called a document. When WordPerfect has been started up, an almost empty screen will
appear and you can now begin to create a new document.

The name of the document you are working on is shown
at the top of the screen, adjacent to the program name
(WordPerfect). In the lower right-hand corner you will
observe:

```
Pg 1 Ln 1" Pos 1"
```

This indicates the position on paper where the cursor
(the blinking stripe showing the current text insertion
point) is located at the moment. That is:

■ Page 1;
■ Line 1", in other words, 1" from the top edge of the
  paper. This is the default upper margin;
■ Position 1", in other words, 1" from the left edge of the
  paper. This is the default setting for the left margin.

Changing the margins is discussed in chapter 7.

3.2   Typing text

You can type the text just as with a typewriter, but you
will soon notice that a word which does not fit into a line
is automatically placed on the next line. This is called
'word wrap'.

If you make a mistake while typing, press Backspace to
remove the letter(s) just typed.

3.2.1   Shift, Caps Lock and NumLock

Using the Shift key, you are able to type capital letters instead of small letters and characters such as ! @ £ $ etc instead of numbers.

The keyboard also has the **Capitals Lock** feature for retaining the capital letters mode. You can switch this feature on and off by pressing the Caps Lock key. When Caps Lock has been switched on (a small lamp in the upper right-hand corner of the keyboard will light up, and in the lower right-hand corner you will see POS instead of Pos), you are able to type capital letters without having to press the Shift key. If you do press the Shift key while the Caps Lock key is on, small letters will be produced. Switching on Caps Lock has no effect on the significance of the keys for numbers and punctuation marks.

There is also the **Numeric Lock** feature on the keyboard. This is switched on and off using the NumLock key. When the feature has been activated, the Num Lock lamp lights up. When NumLock is on, the cursor keys (arrow keys) in the right-hand pad of the keyboard no longer serve to move the cursor, but may be used to enter numbers in the document.

3.3   Paragraphs

If you wish to begin a new paragraph, press Enter. If you wish to indent the first line of a paragraph, press Tab one or more times. If you wish to indent the entire paragraph, do not use Tab, use the Indent function:

m   Click on *Layout* in the menu bar, then *Paragraph*, then *Indent*.

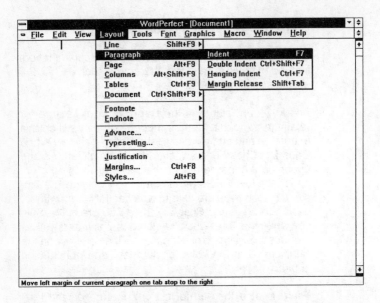

𝒦   Press F7. If you do not always remember which key ac-
        tivates Indent, you can work using the menu. Then
        press Alt-L, R, and I.

𝒟   Press F4.

        In order to place text exactly in the middle of a line, you
        can use the *Centre* function.

𝓜   Click on *Layout*, then *Line*, then *Centre*.

𝒦   Press Shift-F7. If you prefer to work using the menu,
        press Alt-L, L and C.

𝒟   Press Shift-F6.

        If you select *Centre*, all text typed on the same line will
        be positioned in the middle of the line until you press
        Enter. During typing you will see the beginning of the
        text shift to the left.

If you wish to place the text at the end of the line, use the **Flush Right** feature: Alt-F7.

M   Click on *Layout* in the menu bar, then *Line*, then *Flush Right*.

K   Press Alt-F7. If you are not yet familiar with all the key combinations, you can work using menu options. Press Alt-L, then L, then F.

3.4   Bold, underlined and italics

Adjusting the layout and the choice of fonts will be discussed in full later. Nevertheless, when typing the text you may directly wish to specify the words which should be printed bold, underlined or in italics. When typing, the quickest way of doing this is to make use of key combinations or functions keys.

K   Ctrl-B is used to switch the **bold** feature on and off. When you switch on Ctrl-B all subsequent text is made bold until you press Ctrl-B once more, or Ctrl-N (normal).

D   F6 is used to switch the **bold** feature on and off. From the moment you switch the feature on, all subsequent text will be made bold until you press F6 once more.

The same applies to <u>underlining</u>.

K   Press Ctrl-U. Now all subsequent text will be underlined. Press Ctrl-U again or Ctrl-N to return to normal text.

D   Press F8, all subsequent text will be underlined. Press F8 again to switch the function off.

If you use the standard Windows key combinations, you can use the Ctrl-I combination for *italics*. A combination of these keystrokes is also possible to produce ***Bold italics***, *<u>italics underlined</u>* etc. The easiest way or returning to normal text is by pressing Ctrl-N.

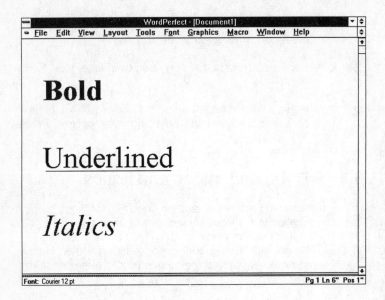

3.5   Deleting text

In general, if you wish to adjust a text which already exists, some parts of it will have to be removed. The most convenient way of doing this depends on the amount of text. If it is only a question of one or two letters (or other characters), proceed as follows:

🄺   Move the cursor using the cursor keys to the first letter you wish to remove. Press Delete until all the letters you wish to remove have been deleted. *Or:* Move the cursor to the first letter or space *behind* the letters you wish to remove and press Backspace until they disappear.

🄼   Click on the first character of the part of the text you wish to remove. Press Delete until all unwanted letters disappear.

If you remove too much text by accident, you can undo this error. Ensure that the cursor is positioned where the deleted text was, otherwise the text will be restored at the wrong place.

M Click on *Edit* in the menu bar, then *Undelete*, then *Restore*.

K Simultaneously press Shift-Alt-Backspace. This can also be done via the menu by choosing Alt-E, N, R.

D Press F3 (the functions F1 and F3 have been switched with respect to the DOS version) and press Enter.

If you wish to remove a larger piece of text, the process works faster if you first select the text. Selected text is often called a *block*, which is why WP users speak of 'making a text block'. The procedure is as follows:

M Click on the starting point of the text you wish to remove. *Select On* will appear in the lower left-hand corner. Drag the mouse to the end point of the section of text. The screen clearly displays the text which has been selected. Press the Delete key to delete this piece of text, or click on *Cut* in the *Edit* menu. If you do this, the deleted text will be stored in the Windows *Clipboard* for the time being. Keep in mind that any text which is already located in the Clipboard will now be removed.

K Place the cursor at the begining of the text which is to be deleted, Press and hold down the Shift key while moving the cursor to the end of the text to be removed. The screen clearly displays the selected block. Then press the Delete key to remove the block.

D Place the cursor at the first letter of the text which is to be removed. Press Alt-F4. Then, using the cursor keys, move the cursor to the first character *after* the text to be deleted. The block is marked. Press Delete or Backspace.

Using the mouse makes it possible to select text quickly:

■ A word is selected by clicking on it twice.
■ By clicking three times on a random spot in a sentence, the whole sentence is selected.
■ By clicking four times on a random spot, the whole paragraph is selected.

The deletion of a word can also take place in another way. Set the cursor on any character in the word (or on the first space behind the word). Then press Ctrl-Backspace. The whole word is deleted including the space behind it. Pay attention to the fact that words having a hyphen between them or a punctuation mark instead of a space are regarded by WordPerfect as being one word and are accordingly also removed when Ctrl-Backspace are pressed.

In addition, there is also another quick method of deleting text from the cursor position to the end of the line. This can be done by pressing Ctrl-Del. Thus, you can remove a whole line by placing the cursor at the beginning of the line and pressing Ctrl-Del. Remember that a *line* is not the same as a *sentence*.

3.6   Inserting or replacing text

The standard setting in WordPerfect is geared to the insertion of text. Place the cursor at a random point in the text and type several words. They are inserted in the existing text, at the spot where you started typing. You can use the *Insert* key to switch between *inserting* and *overtyping*. When you first press the *Insert* key, all then existing text is *replaced* by the new text you now type, beginning at the cursor position. The word **Typeover** is shown in the lower left-hand corner of the screen. If you press Insert once more, you can again *insert* text beginning at the current cursor position.

3.7 Moving the cursor more quickly

Using the cursor keys, you can move the insertion point (the cursor position) through the text in all directions. But there are also other methods using certain key combinations. When moving the cursor, it makes no difference which keyboard definition you use. If you have chosen keyboard definition for the DOS version of WP, there is the option 'Home key as in DOS WP 5.1'. If you do not choose this option, or if you have selected the Windows Keyboard definition (CUA), the key combinations shown below enable you to move the cursor more quickly:

Ctrl-Cursor Right	to the beginning of the next word
Ctrl-Cursor Left	to the beginning of the (previous) word
Ctrl-Cursor Up	to the beginning of the previous paragraph
Ctrl-Cursor Down	to the beginning of the next paragraph
End	to the end of the line, before any codes at the end of the line
End, End	to the end of the line, behind any codes at the end of the line
Home	to the beginning of a line of text (behind any codes at the beginning of the line)
Home, Home	to the beginning of a line (before any codes at the beginning of the line)
Ctrl-Home	to the beginning of a text in a document (behind any codes at the beginning)
Ctrl-Home-Home	to the beginning of a document (before any codes at the beginning)
Ctrl-End	to the end of a document
Page Up	to the top of the screen or move up one screen
Page Down	to the bottom of the screen or move down one screen

Alt-Page Up   to the first line on the (previous page)

Alt-Page Down   to the first line on the next page

Pay attention to the difference: Ctrl-Cursor Right means press both keys *simultaneously*; End, End means press the key *twice in succession*.

3.8   Naming and saving

If you have created a text which you wish to review or edit later, you can save it on the computer harddisk or on a diskette. During installation of WordPerfect the program has asked for specification of the standard directory for documents (text files). However, you may store a document in any chosen directory on any chosen disk.

3.8.1   File names

If you wish to save a document, you have to give it a name. The default setting in WordPerfect, corresponding to that of MS-DOS, requires names of no more than 8 letters (or other valid characters) plus (if desired) an extension of three letters after a full stop. Valid characters are:

- all letters of the alphabet (no difference is made between capitals and small letters)
- the numbers 0 to 9 inclusive
- the signs ! @ # $ % & ( ) _ { } ' ~

Other characters than these are not permitted in file names. WordPerfect itself makes much use of the braces { } for program files and temporary files. Accordingly, it is advisable not to use braces in file names in order to keep a clear distinction between files which belong to WordPerfect and those which you have created yourself.

3.8.2   Saving interim

Perhaps you wish to save a text which is partially complete and continue working on it?

M   Click on *File*, then *Save*. If you have not saved this file
previously, the 'Save As' dialogue box will appear. In
this, the name of a disk (A:, B:, C: etc) and the name of
a directory are already filled in. If you wish to use another directory, enter the complete path, for instance,

```
c:\text\wp\letters\
```

followed by your name for the file. If you wish to use the
standard directory already specified in dialogue box,
you only have to specify the file name. Then click on
Save.

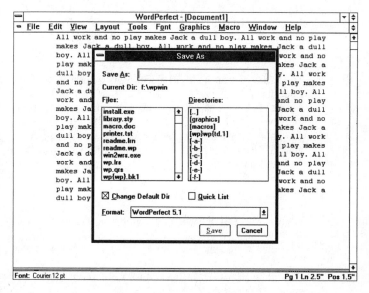

K   Press Shift-F3 **or** first Alt-F and then S. The 'Save As'
dialogue box will appear if the text has not previously
been saved.
Enter the file name. If you do not wish to store it in the

specified default directory, you should enter the complete path to the required directory. Press Tab until the word *Save* is marked and press Enter.

Select *Save* (F10). The 'Save As' dialogue box will appear. Proceed as described above.

If the file has already been saved on disk, WordPerfect will automatically enter the name of the file. You do not need to specify a name.

The WP document is stored in the default document directory, unless you specify otherwise.

Examples

The document directory is called C:\TEXT. You assign the name HUMPHREY.LET to a letter. This file is placed in the C:\TEXT directory. Thus, for DOS, this file is known as C:\TEXT\HUMPHREY.LET.

You assign the name LETTERS\LAUREN.LET to another letter. It is then placed in the directory C:\TEXT\LETTERS. If this directory does not yet exist, you will receive an error message when you enter the name of the file. However, you can easily create a new directory from WordPerfect, as you will learn later in this chapter. For DOS the file can be found under

```
C:\TEXT\LETTERS\LAUREN.LET.
```

In the same situation, you assign the file name

```
C:\CORRESP\RICHLIZ4.LET
```

The file is stored as RICHLIZ4.LET in the directory

```
C:\CORRESP.
```

3.8.3 Saving and ending a document

Do you want to save the completed text?

𝓜 Click on *File*, then *Close*. A dialogue box will appear asking if you wish to save the the alterations in the document. Click on *Yes*.

𝓚 Select *File*, then *Close*: press Ctrl-F4 **or** first press Alt-F then C. A dialogue box will appear with the question whether you wish to save the alterations made. Press Tab until *Yes* is highlighted and press Enter **or** press Y.

𝓓 Select Close: F7. WordPerfect will then ask if you wish to save the altered document. Press Tab until 'Yes' is highlighted and press Enter **or** press Y.

If you have not saved the document previously, Word-Perfect will request a name. The information above dealing with saving a document is also applicable here.

3.9 Making backups

Almost nothing is so frustrating for the computer user as losing a file which has been worked on for a period of time. For this reason, **at least** one backup should be made. Two are even better. The best procedure is to save a file twice or three times each time you discontinue working on a certain file: once on the harddisk and once or twice on diskettes. Neither harddisk nor diskette are always 100% reliable.

Example: you are working on a report which you have called REP_1.FIL. The C:\TEXT directory is the default directory for documents. You wish to save the file on the harddisk and make two backups on diskette.

𝓜 First save the file in the default directory (or in another chosen directory) on C:as described above using *Save*. Then choose *Save As* (from the File menu) and save the file as a:\rep_1.fil.

𝒦   First save the file as described above using *Save* in the
     default directory (or self-chosen directory) on C:. Then
     choose *Save As*, F3, and save the file as a:\rep_1.fil.

𝒟   Select *Save As*: F10 and specify the name rep_1.fil. This
     is saved as C:\TEXT\REP_1.FIL. Then select *Save As*
     (F10) once more and specify the file + path as a:\rep_1.fil.

3.10   Retrieving documents

If you wish to retrieve a document in order to edit it or to
append it to the text which is currently on your screen,
proceed as follows:

𝓜   Click on *File*, then on *Retrieve*.

𝒦   Press Alt-F, then R.

𝒟   When using the DOS WP keyboard, there is no separ-
     ate key combination for *Retrieve* (this is available for
     Open, see below). Press Alt-F to open the File menu
     and then R for Retrieve. A dialogue box will appear:

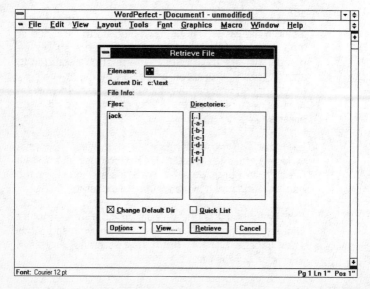

If the document is located in the current document directory, you only need to specify the complete name of the file required. If the document is located in a subdirectory of the document directory, you must specify the names of the directories in between. If neither of these cases is applicable, you must specify the complete path precisely from the diskdrive letter.

Here are some examples in which the default directory for documents is C:\WPTEXT\CORRESP

You wish to retrieve the file C:\WPTEXT\CORRESP\TRITON.FAC. Enter:

```
TRITON.FAC.
```

You wish to retrieve a file with the path + name: C:\WPTEXT\CORRESP\LETTERS\CLINTON.LET. Enter:

```
LETTERS\CLINTON.LET
```

You wish to retrieve the file C:\REPORTS\MARKTANL.RP2. Enter:

```
C:\REPORTS\MARKTANL.RP2
```

You wish to use a file from diskette SURVEY.OLD. Enter

```
A:SURVEY.OLD
```

If you are working with a mouse, there is an easier method. Within the *Retrieve File* dialogue box, there is a box containing Directories. If you wish to move to a higher directory (a parent directory) click on the two points at the top and then on *Retrieve* (or click twice on the two points). If you wish to go to a subdirectory of the current directory, click on the name of the subdirectory and then on *Retrieve* (or click twice on the name). The names of the files contained in the subdirectory will then be shown in the Directories window.

3.11 Opening a file

Opening a file takes place in roughly the same way.

M   Click on *File*, then on *Open*.

K   Press F4, or press Alt-F, O.

D   Press Shift-F10.

The dialogue box 'Open File' resembles that of 'Retrieve File'. The difference is that you can also open a file while already working on another file. A new working window is created for the file newly opened. In this way, it is possible to work on two files at the same time, independent of each other. If required, it is possible to move or copy sections of text from one file to the other. When you have finished working on one of the files, select *Close* from the *File* menu and the corresponding window will be closed. The WordPerfect program will not yet be closed as is the case when you use *Exit*.

3.12 Working on two or more documents simultaneously

If you are working on a certain document, you can use the *Open* option discussed above to open another window with a different document. How are the two files displayed simultaneously?

M   Click on the *Restore* sizing button in the top right-hand corner of the document window, next to the menu bar, *not* next to the title bar. The window decreases in size and behind it the window of the other document becomes partially visible.

Using the mouse, you can drag the title bar, if required, over the screen. In this way, you take the entire window with you. By clicking on the title bar of the one of the other document it is drawn to the foreground where you can work on it.

🅺 Press Alt-W. Choose *Cascade* or *Tile* by typing C or T. You can switch between documents by typing Alt-W and then typing the number of the required document.

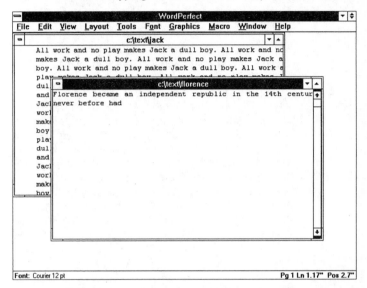

When you have finished working on one of the files,

🅼 ensure that the file you wish to close is the active file (see the colour of the title bar, it should be dark). Click on *File*, then *Close*.

🅺 ensure that the document you wish to close is active (see the colour of the title bar, it should be dark). Press Ctrl-F4.

🅳 ensure that the document you wish to close is active. Press F7.

3.13   Specifying a different default directory

Temporarily

You can change the default directory for documents in two ways. If you wish to do this temporarily, i.e. as long as WordPerfect is active, proceed as follows:

𝓶   Click on *File*, then on *Retrieve* or *Open*. In the dialogue box which subsequently appears on your screen, by clicking on the two points (..) and then on *Retrieve* or *Open*, you can move to the parent directories. By clicking on the required directory name in the list of subdirectories and then on *Retrieve* or *Open*, you activate the following subdirectory. If a cross is located in the check box next to 'Change Default Dir', this becomes the new default directory until you close WPWin. You can place or remove a cross in the corresponding box by clicking on it. If there is no cross, the default directory will remain the same.

𝓚   Press Alt-F and then O or R. Press Tab twice in order to move to the list of directories. Select a directory using the Cursor Up and Cursor Down keys. The two points represent a higher directory and the directory names refer to subdirectories of the current directory. Press Tab again to move to the 'Change Default Dir' option. If a cross is shown here, the directory now chosen will become the default directory until you close WPWin or specify another. If no cross is shown here, the default directory will remain unchanged. You can set or remove a cross by pressing the spacebar. Press Tab four times so that 'Open' or 'Retrieve' is highlighted, then press Enter.

Permanently

If you wish to change the default directory for a longer period of time, so that the change is valid each time you activate WordPerfect for Windows, you should do this via the Installation.

M   Click on *File*, then *Preferences*, then *Location of Files*. Click on the box next to 'Documents' and specify the name of the required new default directory. The path to the directory must be accurately specified from C:\ (or D:\, F:\ etc). Click on OK. If you wish to search for a directory name, click on the list button to the right of the 'Documents' box. A dialogue box will then appear containing a list as described above concerning Opening and Retrieving files.

K   Press Alt-F, then type E, then L. Press Tab to move to the 'Documents' box. Specify the required directory name (the entire path from the root directory), then press Enter.

D   Press F1, then L. Press Tab to move to the 'Documents' box. Specify the required directory name (the entire path from the root directory). Press Enter.

3.14   Typing special characters

There are many characters for which there is no special key on the keyboard. For instance, in French ç and ê, in German ü and ß, in Spanish ñ and ì, to name but a few from the most common languages. If you have to type text from East or North European languages, it becomes even more complicated.

3.14.1   Using the Alt key

Just how do you type an ë, for example? WordPerfect 4.2 and previous versions had only one solution to this problem: hold down the Alt key and type the number 137 using the numeric keypad at the right-hand side of the keyboard. 137 is the value for the ë character in the so-called *ASCII set*. Using the Alt key, you can type all the values in this set of computer characters, also in programs other than WordPerfect. In DOS versions of

WP, it makes no difference whether NumLock is switched on or not. In WPWin, you can also enter all the ASCII values using the Alt key, but NumLock **must** be switched on. (The NumLock lamp clearly shows this.) ANSI characters which do not correspond to ASCII characters cannot be made using Alt key combinations, i.e. the values 001 to 032 inclusive cannot be used. You can summon the corresponding characters from the ANSI character set using the menu (see below).

3.14.2   Using the character set

Looking up tables is no longer necessary in WordPerfect for Windows.
For instance, how do you type an ñ?

Click on *Font*, then on *WP Characters*. The dialogue box for WordPerfect character fonts appears.

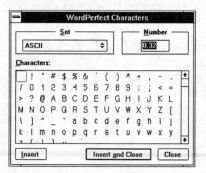

Press Ctrl-W **or** first Alt-O, then W. The WordPerfect character dialogue box appears.
In the upper left-hand corner, the set name will appear, e.g. ASCII. To the right of this, a number is displayed, e.g. 0.32. This number indicates which number can be chosen at this moment: character set nr. 0, character nr. 32. The large area underneath displays the characters from the corresponding set. If it is an extensive set, only a part of the set will be visible.

Perhaps you wish to choose another set?

𝓂   Click on the name which is displayed next to 'Set' and hold down the left mouse button. A list of character set names will appear. Move through this list until the required set is highlighted, then release the mouse button.

𝓚   Ensure that the name of the set is marked. (If that is not the case, press Tab until you reach the proper option.) Press Cursor Down and/or Cursor Up until the required set is able to be selected. Each time the name of a set appears, the corresponding characters are displayed in the middle window.

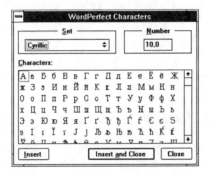

If not all characters from a set are visible, proceed as follows:

𝓂   Click on the arrows in the scroll bars at the right of the window to draw different rows of characters step by step into the display.

𝓚   Press (if the set name is not yet highlighted) Tab twice to move into the character window. By moving the cursor downwards (it now has the form of a square enclosing a character), you make the next row of characters visible.

If you wish to examine the characters more closely, you can press the control menu button (in the upper left-hand corner of the dialogue box) and select 'Size' which allows you to enlarge the frame. Move the position of the upper left-hand corner upwards and/or to the left. The characters will be shown larger on the screen and more characters will be displayed on the screen at one time. This can be very useful particularly in cases when you need many special characters. When you see the required character, mark it using the cursor keys.

There are three options at the bottom of the dialogue box: Insert, Insert and Close, and Close. If you wish to insert the chosen character in the text and you think you will require more special characters, select Insert. The frame containing the character sets will remain on the screen. If you do not wish to use the character, select Close. The dialogue box disappears.

If you select Insert and Close, the character is inserted at the current cursor position in the text, and the dialogue box disappears from the screen. You can make this selection by:

ℳ   Clicking on one of the three options.

𝒦   Using Tab to move to your choice and pressing Enter, or by pressing the underlined letter in the required option.

Accordingly, you can type symbols such as © § and Greek, Hebrew and Cyrillian (Russian) characters. By the way, printing texts in which these characters occur takes considerably longer than printing texts which only contain printer standard characters. This also depends to a certain extent on the printer.

3.14.3   Overstrike: making your own characters

It may be quicker to create your own characters than to search for them in the character sets. For example, do you wish to type an ë? Press Ctrl-W, then type inverted commas, then an e and press Enter. Using this procedure, the character set dialogue box will be displayed, but you do not have to search for the character. Word-Perfect is acquainted with the following combinations which you can produce yourself:

■ letters with a tilde or umlaut by combining the letter and inverted commas;

■ letters with an acute accent (é, ú, á) by combining the letter and one inverted comma;

■ letters with grave accent, by using the ' which is generally located in the upper left corner of the keyboard;

■ the C cedilla (Ç, ç) by typing small or capital C with a comma;

■ the Dutch guilder sign (*f*) using an f with a dash;

■ the ß (Ringel s) using two times s;

■ the œ by typing o and e, the æ by typing a and e.

■ the ñ by typing a tilde ~ (mostly upper left of the keyboard) and an n;

■ the å by typing an o and an a;

■ the Ø and ø by typing a slash and a small or capital O;

■ the fractions ½ and ¼ using a slash and the 2 or 4 as required.

3.15   Searching for text

The following could occur: you have typed a long text and you wish to insert something into it but the place where the new text should be inserted cannot be found quickly. You know, of course, what the text was discussing at that point: a *tennis ball*, and you only used those words once in the entire text. In that case, it won't be difficult to find. First go to the beginning of the document: Press Ctrl-Home.
Now search for the words 'tennis ball' as follows:

M   Click on *Edit* in the menu bar, then *Search*. Specify the words **tennis ball** in the text box. Click on *Search*.

K   Press F2, or first Alt-E, then S. Specify the required words in the text box. Press Enter.

Searching backwards is also possible. You are busy
typing a text and you think you have used the word 'be-
havior', with the American spelling of the word. Was that
so or not? Let's look and see.

ℳ   Click on *Edit* in the menu bar, then *Search*. Specify the
word **behavio**. (The last letter has been deliberately
omitted, then WP will find either version.) Click on *Forwards*, hold down the mouse button and move to *Backwards*. Release the button. Click on *Search*.

𝒦   Press F2, or first Alt-E, then S. Specify the part of the
word of which you are sure: **behavio**. Press Tab twice
to highlight *Forwards*. Press B to change this to *Backwards*. Press Tab twice to highlight *Search*. Press
Enter.

3.16   Searching for codes

You can also look for codes. Imagine you have typed a
report consisting of many pages of text and you wish to
examine whether everything has been set down in a
logical order of sequence and nothing important has
been forgotten. A heading in bold letters has been assigned to each section of the report. In order to review
the headings quickly one after the other, proceed as follows:

ℳ   Go to the beginning of the text by dragging the button in
the scroll bar at the right-hand side of the screen completely to the top. Click on *Edit*, then on *Search*. A dialogue box will appear. Click on *Codes*. A separate window containing a list of codes will be displayed. Click on
the arrows at the bottom of the scroll bar until the *Bold
On* code is visible. Click on this code, then on *Insert*. In
the Search dialogue box, **[Bold On]** has been placed in
the text box. Click on *Search*.

𝒦   Go to the beginning of the text. Press F2. The Search
dialogue box appears. Press Alt-C to select *Codes*. A
window containing a list of codes is displayed. Press

Cursor Down until *Bold On* is highlighted. Press Enter. The code **[Bold On]** is placed in the text box. Press Alt-S to select Search. In order to move to the following point where the **[Bold On]** code has been used, you only need to press Shift-F2.

3.17   Search and replace

A feature which you will probably use frequently is **search and replace**. This enables you to replace a word (or something else which often recurs) with another word or codes. This can be done throughout the entire text or only at places which you indicate. We shall illustrate this using a couple of examples.

Imagine you have typed a three-page letter. The letter contains a large number of paragraphs. At the end of each paragraph, you pressed Enter once, and you began a new paragraph. In retrospect, you would rather have a blank line between the paragraphs. The solution is simple: move the cursor to the first line, and replace Enter with two times Enter. Thus, first go to the beginning of the document.

M   Click on *Edit*, then *Replace*. A dialogue box appears. The cursor is located next to 'Search For:'. The abbreviation HRt (for Hard Return) should be specified here. Click on *Codes*. Click on the arrow in the lower right-hand corner of the box containing the list of codes until *[HRt]* appears. Click on this code.

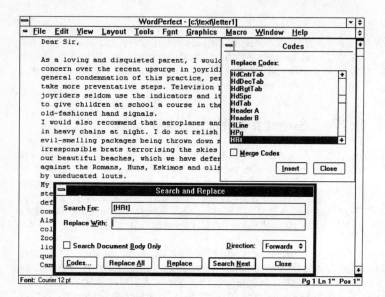

Now click in the text box next to 'Replace With:'. In the code list, *HRt* is still highlighted. Click twice on *Insert*. Click on *Replace All*.

Press Ctrl-F2. A dialogue box appears. Press Alt-C to select *Codes*. The box containing the list of codes is shown. Press the arrow keys until *HRt* is visible. Press Enter. The [HRt] code is placed in the 'Search For:' text box. Press Tab to move to the other text box. Press Alt-C to move to the Codes box. **HRt** is still highlighted. Press Enter in order to place this code in the 'Replace With:' box. Again press Alt-C and the Enter. Press Alt-A to select *Replace All*. Press Esc to close the window.

Press Alt-F2. A dialogue box is displayed. Proceed as described above.

Imagine you have to type a text in which the term 'Laid Out Rudderless Drinking Society' frequently occurs. In order to lighten the workload, you type only the letters **lords** each time. When the entire text has been typed, you will replace *lords* with *Laid Out Rudderless Drinking*

Society. Working in this way not only saves a great deal of actual typing, it drastically reduces the risk of typing errors, if you ensure that it is done once perfectly. When the text is completed, and the abbreviation *lords* appears throughout the text, move the cursor to the beginning of the text and proceed as follows:

M Click on *Edit*, then on *Replace*. Behind 'Search For:' specify **lords** and then click in the 'Replace With:' box. Specify the words **Laid Out Rudderless Drinking Society**. Click on *Replace All*. Click on *Close*.

K Press Ctrl-F2. Specify **lords** in the upper text box. Press Tab, specify **Laid Out Rudderless Drinking Society** in the other text box. Press Alt-A (Replace All). Press Esc.

D Press Alt-F2 and proceed as described above.

Imagine that a text created in WordPerfect for a brochure will be given a certain format using a DTP program. The paragraph headings, which you had underlined, receive a special layout and you have been requested to remove the underlining. The quickest way of doing this is to move the cursor to the beginning of the text and then to replace the **Undrln** code with nothing. Proceed as follows:

M Click on *Edit*, then *Replace*. Click on *Codes* in the dialogue box. Click on the arrow at the bottom of the scroll bar in the codes window, until **Undrln** appears. Click on *Undrln*, click on *Insert*. Click in the 'Replace With:' box and remove any text or code which may be present. Click on *Replace All*. Click on *Close*.

K Press Ctrl-F2. Press Alt-C. Press the Cursor Down key until **Undrln** is highlighted. Press Enter. Press Tab to move to the 'Replace With:' box and remove any text or codes which may be present. Press Alt-A. Press Esc.

D Press Alt-F2. Proceed as described above (from Press Alt-C).

3.18   Working with blocks of selected text

Selecting text and then moving, deleting, copying or editing it in any way can save a great deal of effort. How
does this work exactly?

3.18.1   Selecting

M   Place the pointer at the beginning of the text you wish to
select. Drag it to the end of the section of text by holding
down the left mouse button and moving the pointer. Release the mouse button when the whole section of text
has been selected.

K   Place the cursor at the beginning of the section of text
you wish to select. Press Shift and hold it down while
moving the cursor to the end of the section of text using
the cursor keys or Page Down (if the text is lengthy).
Only release Shift when the cursor is stationary.

D   Place the cursor at the beginning of the required block
of text. Press Alt-F4. Move the cursor to the end of the
section of text you wish to select.

The selected text can be recognized by the inverse
video display.

3.18.2   Deleting

Selected text can be deleted by pressing Del. If this occurs unintentionally, you can still recover the text:

M   Click on *Edit*, click on *Undelete*. This command lets you
restore any of the last three deletions.

K   Press Alt-Shift-Backspace.

D   Press F3.

3.18.3 Moving

Do you wish to move the selected text?

M   Click on *Edit*, then *Cut*. Move the cursor to the place where you wish the text to be inserted. Click on *Edit*, then *Paste*.

K   Press Shift-Del. Move the cursor to the place where the text should be inserted. Press Shift-Insert.

3.18.4 Copying

Do you wish to copy the selected text?

M   Click on *Edit*, then *Copy*. Move the cursor to the place where you wish to place the same text. Click on *Edit*, then *Paste*.

K   Press Ctrl-Ins. Move the cursor to the place where you wish to place the same text. Press Shift-Ins.

3.18.5 Moving or copying to another document

Importing a text into another document is easy. Select the text and specify whether the text block should be moved (Shift-Del) or copied (Ctrl-Ins). Open the other document or, if it has already been opened, activate the relevant window. Place the cursor at the required position in the new document and select *Paste* (Shift-Ins).

3.18.6 Saving a text block as a file

You can also save blocks of text separately. Select a block as described above. In the *File* menu select the *Save As* option. The *Save Selected Text* box appears on the screen. Specify the name you wish to assign to the text block. Click on *Save* or press Enter.

3.18.7   Deselection

Do you wish to undo a selection?

𝓜   Click on a spot outside the selected text.

𝓚   Move the cursor without pressing Shift.

𝓓   Press Alt-F4.

3.18.8   Conversion to capitals or small letters

You are able to convert an entire section of text to small
or capital letters in one go. Select the text as described
above.

𝓜   Click on *Edit*, then on *Convert Case*, then on *Uppercase*
         or *Lowercase*.

𝓚   Press Alt-E, then O, then U or L.

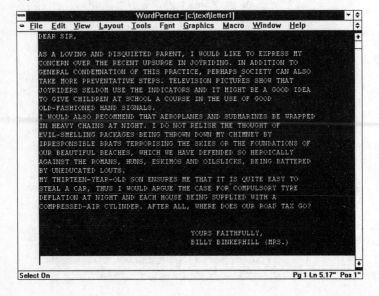

Exercises

1. Type the following text without making use of the WP character sets:

    Mist over Channel: Continent isolated
    Thick mist over the Channel yesterday
    prevented any shipping contact with
    the Continent. Sir Billy Binkerhill,
    MP for Dochester, expressed his
    concern. "My first inclinations are
    humanitarian," he stated. He went on
    to say, "Perhaps we should send a
    peace-keeping force in case the
    blighters across there begin running
    amok. We have holiday homes in Béziers
    and Nîmes." The Home Secretary, who
    was lunching with his mistress, was
    not available for comment.

    Save this document under the name REPORT and clear the screen.

2. Type the following text. Create the special characters, do not extract them from the WP character sets:

            Through the looking glasses
    Despite any animosity on the field,
    there is no trace of ill-feeling in
    everyday life. On the contrary, the
    formal rivals have several mutual
    interests. Charlton is fond of a nip
    of Irish whiskey, while Müller and
    Rußman are not averse to a good glass
    of Löwenbrau.

    Save this document under the name GLASS and clear the screen.

Procedures

1. Ctrl-B switches on the bold feature. Type the head-
    ing and switch the bold feature off by pressing Ctrl-
    B again or Ctrl-N. Now ensure that NumLock is on.
    If the small lamp is not lit, press NumLock once.
    Special characters can be generated by holding
    down the Alt key and pressing the numbers in the
    numeric keypad at the right of the keyboard. The é
    is produced by pressing Alt-130 and the î is made
    by pressing Alt-140.
    When the text is complete, select *Save As* from the
    File menu, specify the name REPORT, click on
    Save or press Enter, and select *Close* from the *File*
    menu.

2. First type the text, without centring the heading. To
    produce the ü, press Ctrl-W, inverted commas,
    then u. For the ß, press Ctrl-W, s,s, then press
    Enter. For the ö, press Ctrl-W, inverted commas, o,
    then press Enter.
    To centre the heading, select *Layout, Justification,
    Centre*. A tick mark is placed in front of *Centre*.
    When the text has been centred, repeat the proce-
    dure to switch the justification off again.
    When the text is completed, Press Alt-F and select
    Save As. Specify the name GLASS and press
    Enter. Select *File* and *Close*.

4 Language functions

4.1 Hyphenation

If you have activated hyphenation in the *Line Hyphenation* dialogue box (*Layout, Line, Hyphenation*), words which do not fit into one line are automatically hyphenated by WordPerfect. If long words, with which WordPerfect is not familiar, occur in a text, the program will ask where the hyphen should be placed, by means of a dialogue box. If this function is not activated, go to the *File* menu and select *Preferences, Environment, Prompt for Hyphenation*. Now choose 'When Required' by clicking on the option or by moving to it using the Tab and cursor keys and pressing Enter.

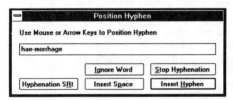

Using the cursor keys, you can move the position of the hyphen in the word. You can also click with the mouse at the position where you wish the hyphenation to come. When the hyphenation is as you wish it to be, click on *Insert Hyphen* or press Enter.

It may occur that there is no suitable point to hyphenate the word. In that case, click on *Ignore Word* or press Esc.

Other possibilities are: hyphenation with a *soft return (SRt)* or inserting a space. In both cases, the sections of the word will be split over the two lines, but at the end of the first line, no hyphen will be shown.

4.1.1   Hyphenation off

Perhaps you do not want hyphenation in your document?

M   Click on *Layout*, then *Line*, then *Hyphenation*. The *Line Hyphenation* dialogue box will appear. Click on the cross in the 'Hyphenation On' box. It will disappear. Click on OK.

K   Press Shift-F9, then E. A dialogue box will appear. Press Tab twice. Press the spacebar so that the cross in the 'Hyphenation On' box disappears. Press Enter.

D   Press Shift-F8, then L, then E. A dialogue box will appear. Press Tab twice. Press the spacebar so that the cross in the 'Hyphenation On' box disappears. Press Enter.

If you subsequently decide that you would prefer hyphenation, proceed as above. This will lead to a cross being placed in the 'Hyphenation On' box.

4.1.2   Specifying the hyphenation zone

In the Line Hyphenation dialogue box, you can also specify in which cases hyphenation should be applied. (If there is no cross next to 'Hyphenation On' this will, of course, not occur.) The hyphenation zone is normally 10% left and 4% right. Words which start before the left side and extend beyond the right side are candidates for hyphenation.
The hyphenation zone depends on the length of the line. WordPerfect calculates 10% of the line length and uses that for the distance from the left edge of the hyphenation zone to the right margin. WordPerfect uses 4% of the line length to determine the right side of the hyphenation zone (which is only used when Full Justification is on - more about this later).
The longer the line, the larger the hyphenation zone. When the hyphenation zone is larger, fewer words

cross both boundaries and less hyphenation occurs. If you have shorter lines, as is the case with columns of text, the hyphenation zone is smaller and more words are hyphenated. If you want more hyphenation, make the hyphenation zone smaller. For less hyphenation, enlarge the hyphenation zone.

4.2   Spelling check

However well we try to type texts, a mistake is easily made. In order to remove as many mistakes as possible in a straightforward way, WordPerfect provides a spelling check. This compares a section of text or an entire document to an extensive list of words.

The options are:

■ *Word*: checks only the word at the current position of the cursor;
■ *Document*: the entire document undergoes a spelling check;
■ *To End of Document*: checks document from current position of the cursor to the end;
■ *Page*: checks the page where the cursor is currently positioned, thus not the previous or next pages;
■ *To End of Page*: checks page from current position of the cursor to the end.

If a block of text has been selected, this can also be checked.

In addition, there are the following options under Options:

Words with Numbers:
        if the speller encounters a word with numbers, you must indicate whether this is deliberate;
Duplicate Words:
        if two identical words are located next to each other, the speller asks if this is correct;

Irregular Capitalization:
the speller will ask for confirmation if capitals
occur at an unexpected place - mainly when small
letters are followed by a capital letter with no
space between.

One option which only refers to the screen display is
'Move to Bottom'. This enables you to move the Speller
window to the bottom of the screen.

How do you check a typed text?

M   Click on *Tools*, then *Speller*. A dialogue box appears.
Click on the options button next to 'Check' if you do not
wish to check the entire document. Make a selection.
By clicking on *Options* and on one of the options there,
you can specify how the check should take place. Click
on *Start*. As soon as a word is found which does not
occur in the list of words, the dialogue box will alter.

The unknown word is displayed in the small 'Word' window. You can change it one letter at a time. If there are
words in the word list which resemble this word, they
are displayed in the 'Suggestions' window. If the correct
word is also shown here, click on it and then on *Replace*. If the word which has been queried by the Speller
is nevertheless the proper word, click on *Skip Once*. If
this word occurs several times in the text, it is better to
click on *Skip Always*, otherwise it will be presented
again shortly. If a word has been typed correctly, and
you wish to have it accepted by the Speller in other documents as well, click on *Add*. (In the case of words
which rarely occur, it is better not to add them to the
word list since this will slow down future spelling
checks.) When you wish to stop working with the Speller, click on *Close*.

K   Press Ctrl-F1. (You can also activate the Speller using
the menu: Alt-T, then S.) A dialogue box will appear. If
you do not wish to check the entire document, press
Tab so that you can select the range you wish to have
checked. If you wish to switch certain options on or off,

Press Alt-P and type the first letter of the option you wish to alter. Press Enter in order to start the spelling check.

If an 'unknown' word is found, the Speller will display it in the 'Word' box. You can change it yourself. To do this, press Tab once and then you may make the alteration. If there are words in the standard list which resemble the unknown word, these are shown in the 'Suggestions' box. If the word you require is shown there, correctly spelled, you can highlight it by moving the cursor keys (if no word is marked, press Tab until this is the case) and replace the wrong word by pressing Tab three times and then pressing R for Replace.

If the found word is nevertheless as it should be, press Tab until one of the boxes in the bottom row is highlighted. Type O in order to select the *Skip Once* option. If the word occurs more than once in the text, type an L for *Skip Always*. If you wish to add a word to the standard list since it also occurs in other documents, type an A for *Add*. When you wish to stop working with the Speller, press Tab until *Close* is marked and then press Enter.

🖙 Press Ctrl-F2. Proceed further as described above.

4.3 Spelling and grammatical check in foreign languages

Spelling check in languages other than English can only be done if you acquire other language modules in addition to the language module supplied along with the English version of WPWin. WordPerfect has language modules for (UK, Australian, Canadian, US) English, Czech, Danish, Dutch, French, German, Greek, Italian, Norwegian, Polish, Russian, Swedish, Spanish, Turkish and several other languages. New language modules become available regularly. We shall return shortly to the topic of language modules.

Another possibility is working with a special program for grammatical check. Generally, this also includes a spelling check. Programs such as these are only available for a limited number of languages. The *Grammar* program provides the most possibilities. There are English, American English, French, German and Spanish versions of this program. In the case of the English versions, there is both a DOS version and a Windows version available. The program costs more than a language module for WordPerfect, but provides an exceptionally good spelling check and an excellent grammatical check. Roughly half of all grammatical errors are detected which is a high score. This is only exceeded by the *PowerEdit* program which, however, only provides a grammatical check without a spelling check. PowerEdit is only available for (American) English, as are the programs *The Complete Writer's Toolkit* and *Correct Grammar*, which both provide spelling and grammatical checks. A Windows version of *Correct Grammar* is also on the market now. (See also the Software Indicator, appendix E.)

If you use WordPerfect for translation purposes, you can gain ready assistance from the electronic dictionaries which are now available. These can be easily activated from the word processing program in most cases. (See also the Software Indicator, appendix E.)

4.4   Language modules

The language modules available for WordPerfect have been mentioned above. In general, they contain a hyphenation routine and a Speller for the language in question, and often a Thesaurus. If you were to use the English version of WordPerfect with a Spanish language module, the menus would appear on the screen in English as normal but the program would use the Spanish rules with respect to hyphenation, spelling check etc.

Additional language modules are installed via Install which you have aleady used to install WordPerfect. If you wish to install a language module, select the option 'Install other WordPerfect language modules'. In order to activate another language module during word processing, proceed as follows:

M   Click on *Tools*, then *Language*. A list of languages is shown. Click on the scroll bar arrows next to the Language window if you wish to see the other languages. Double click on the language of your choice.

K   Press Alt-T, then L. Use Cursor Up and Cursor Down to move through the list of languages. Highlight the required language and press Enter.

A code is placed in the text which indicates that you are working in the corresponding language from that point onwards. You can view the codes by pressing Alt-F3.

You can include codes for various languages in one document. From the position where WordPerfect encounters a language code, it refers to the corresponding language for determination of hyphenation routine. If you check the spelling, WordPerfect will examine the relevant language word list in accordance with the current code. Of course, this can only take place if the corresponding language modules have actually been installed.

4.5   Looking for synonyms

When you are busy typing a text, it often occurs that you cannot come up with the appropriate word. WordPerfect provides useful assistance here: the Thesaurus. This provides not only synonyms (words with roughly the same meaning) for the word you have specified, but also words with a related significance, and occasionally antonyms (opposite meaning) as well.

For instance, you have typed:

He was particularly enthusiastic. His reaction, in fact, was so enthusiastic that he ...

Now you realize that you have used the word *enthusiastic* twice within such a short space. You would prefer to use another word, but which? Place the cursor on the second 'enthusiastic' (on any letter) and activate the Thesaurus:

M   Click on *Tools* in the menu bar, then *Thesaurus*. Under *enthusiastic* you will see the words, 'ardent, eager, fervent, rhapsodic, spirited, zealous'. A point is next to some words. If you click on *ardent* and then on *Search* you will then be presented with a new list of words. If you wish to use one of these words to replace *enthusiastic*, click on the appropriate word and then on *Replace*. If you cannot find a suitable word, click on *Close*.

M   Press Alt-F1. (Or, using the menu, first press Alt-T, then T.) A list of synonyms for the corresponding word will be displayed. Press Tab several times and then Cursor Down to highlight a word. If you click on *ardent* and then on *Search*, you will be presented with a new list of words. In order to replace a word in the original text with a new word, press Alt-R. When you wish to discontinue the search for a synonym, press Alt-C to close the window.

Exercises

1. Type the text below exactly as shown:

```
The Final Stage.
The mole rat is a specially
interesting phenomenon. This small
mammal, living in narrow tunnels under
the ground, does not reproduce as
other mamals do, in other words, with
a certain amount of competition
between individuals which ensures the
survival of the fittest. The mole rat
has a Euro-genetic system, like
termites for instance, which supports
the genetic survival of the colony as
```

a whole. In this, the *queen* plays the
central role. Although her offspring
are male or female, they will not pair
as long as they are in the colony and
the queen remains healthy. When they
are set apart from the rest of the
colony, the female becomes 30% longer
which allows her to carry young in the
narrow tunnels.
Some evolutionary theorists see this
as evidence that the socio-genetic
struture of mammals in general, and
thus mankind in particular, may not be
quite so fundamental as it was
previously estimated to be. This is,
of course, fuel for the discussion
concerning DNA applications. Has
mankind reached the final stage in
genetic development?'

Have the text checked for spelling. Save the document under the name GENETIC and clear the
screen.

2.   Open the GENETIC document. Using the Thesaurus, look for alternative words for 'phenomenon'
and colony. Close the document without saving it.

Procedures

1.   Type the text. Click on *Tools*, then on *Speller* (or
press Alt-T, S; or press Ctrl-F1)). Click on the *Start*
button in the *Speller* window (or press the underlined letter). The word **mamal** is displayed. 'mama',
'mammas', 'mammal', 'mumble' are suggested as
correct words. Choose 'mammal' and click on *Replace* (or press R). **Socio-genetic** will then be
found and a number of suggestions will be made,
including 'psycho' and 'saucy'. Nevertheless the
word is correct so select *Skip Once* or *Skip Always*.
Then **struture** will be found. The suggestions are

'structure', straighter', 'strider'. Select 'structure' and *Replace*. The rest of the text is in order. Select *Close*.

2. Click on *File*, then *Retrieve* or *Open* (Alt-F, R or O). Double click on the name 'genetic' (or use cursor keys and Enter). Place the cursor on the word **phenomenon**. Click on *Tools*, *Thesaurus*. A number of alternatives will be given, including **occurrence** and **sensation** but these are not really suitable. Click on *Close*. Place the cursor on **colony** and activate the Thesaurus once more. Again a number of alternatives are shown. If they are not easily legible, click once on each of them - they will appear in the text box at the bottom right of the screen. The word **group** provides the correct significance. Highlight the word and click on *Replace* (press R). The word is replaced. Click on *File, Close, No* (Alt-F, C, N).

5 Special Functions

5.1 Macros

The macro function in WordPerfect can be extremely useful. A series of keystrokes can be stored in a macro. Especially when identical text has to be regularly typed, or the same formatting features used, storing these in a macro can save a great deal of time.

5.1.1 Creating macros

We shall use the closing lines of a letter as an example. We shall make macros for the text *Yours faithfully,* followed by a number of hard returns (to leave space for your signature) and your name in type. We shall also create a macro for the text *With best wishes,* again followed by open space and your name.

We shall begin with the macro for *Yours faithfully.* You must assign a name to the macro. Choose a short name which clearly indicates which kind of macro it is. If you create a number of macros, you should take care that the name is not too short otherwise this may lead to confusion. You can call this macro **YOURS** or **FAITH**.

M   Click on *Macro* in the menu bar, then *Record*. The 'Record Macro' box appears.

You must first assign a name to the macro. Allocate a suitable name of not more than 8 letters. If you wish to add a description, click on the *Descriptive Name* box and enter a short description. You may enter a longer explanation of what the macro does in the *Abstract* box. Click on *Record*. The message *Recording Macro* is displayed at the bottom of the screen.

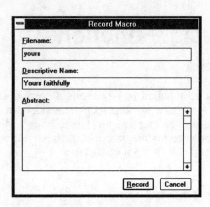

Type the text **Yours faithfully,** press Enter four or five times (the result of the macro is shown immediately on your screen) and type your name. Click again on *Macro* and now on *Stop*.

Press Ctrl-F10, or first on Alt-M, then R. Assign a suitable name (maximum 8 letters) to the macro. If you wish to add a Descriptive Name and/or an Abstract, go to the relevant box using the Tab key and type the appropriate text. When you have done this, press Enter. The message *Recording Macro* will appear at the bottom of your screen. Type the text **Yours faithfully,** press Enter four or five times (the result of the macro is shown immediately on the screen) and type your name. Now press Ctrl-Shift-F10, or Alt-M then S.

Making a macro for **With best wishes,** should present no problems. Depending on how short you wish to make the name, you can call it **Close** or **Bestwish** or whatever you like.

Click on *Macro* in the menu bar, then *Record*. Enter a name and description if you wish. Click on *Record*. Type the text **With best wishes,** press Enter four or five times (the result of the macro is displayed immediately on the screen), and type your name. Click on *Macro* and then *Stop*.

𝒦   Press Ctrl-F10 or Alt-M, R. Assign a name to the macro and a description if required. Press Enter. Type the text **With best wishes,** press Enter four or five times (the result of the macro is shown immediately on the screen), and type your name. Press Ctrl-Shift-F10, or Alt-M, S.

The following example illustrates how you can combine text and layout codes in one macro. We shall create a macro containing your name address and telephone number. Your name will be printed bold and the telephone number in italics. Moreover, the phone number will be preceded by a graphic symbol which can be found in the fifth WordPerfect character set.

𝓂   Click on *Macro* in the menu bar, then *Record*. Assign a name to the macro, for example **ADDRESS**, and click on *Record*. Type your name. Drag the mouse over the line containing your name. Click on *Font* then on *Bold*. Place the cursor at the end of the line once more and press Enter. Type the house number and street and press Enter. Type the postal code and town and press Enter. If you prefer to have a blank line between the address and telephone number, press Enter twice. We shall now look for the telephone symbol. Click on *Font*, then *WP characters*. Choose set 5 (various symbols) symbol 30 (telephone), click on *Insert and Close*. Type one or two spaces (see how it looks on the screen) and then the telephone number. Drag the mouse over the phone number. Click on *Font*, then *Italics*. If you wish to move the cursor to a new line after the telephone number, press Enter. Click on *Macro*, then *Stop*.

𝒦   Press Ctrl-F10. Allocate a name to the macro, for example, **ADDRESS** and press Enter. Press Ctrl-B, type your name and press Ctrl-N. Press Enter. Type the house number and street, press Enter. Type the postal code and town, press Enter. If you prefer to have a blank line between the address and telephone number, press Enter twice. We shall now look for the telephone symbol. Press Ctrl-W, press Cursor Down until set 5 (various symbols) is visible, press Tab twice, highlight

symbol 30 (telephone) using the cursor keys and press
Tab until 'Insert and Close' is marked and press Enter.
Type one or two spaces (see how it looks on the
screen), press Ctrl-I and type the phone number. Press
Ctrl-N. If you wish to have the cursor move to a new line
after the telephone number, press Enter. Press Ctrl-
Shift-F10.

More examples and tips concerning macros are given in
the following chapters.

5.1.2   Running macros

Macros can be assigned to a menu, a button bar or a
key combination. This will be dealt with in the subsequent chapters. However, you can also run any
macro without having to allocate it:

M   Click on *Macro*, then *Play*. Select the required macro in
the Files box, then click on *Play*. You can also double
click on the name of the macro to run it.

K   Press Alt-F10. Move to the File box using the cursor
keys, select the required macro or type the name of the
macro in the Filename box. Select Play and press
Enter.

The first time you run a macro, you will see a message
on the screen that the macro is being *compiled*. This
consumes a little time but ensures that the macro runs
even quicker in the future.

5.1.3   Assigning a macro to the menu

It is possible to assign macros which you have created
yourself (or bought) to the menu. A maximum of 9 macros can be placed in the list under the 'Macro' option in
the menu bar. In order to add the ADDRESS macro, for
instance, to the menu, proceed as follows:

M   Click on *Macro*, then *Assign to Menu*. A Menu Text window will appear. If macros have already been allocated to the menu, their names will be shown in this box. To add a macro to this list, click on *Insert*. The *Insert Macro Menu Item* window will appear. Type the name of the macro, **ADDRESS** in the *Macro Name* box. If this macro is not located in the default directory for macros, type the complete path in front of the macro name. Click on the *Menu Text* box and type a short description of the macro (e.g. name, address, phone). This is the text which will be added to the menu and which allows you to recognize the macro quickly. Click on *OK*.

K   Press Alt-M, then A. The Menu Text window will appear containing the names of the macros which are already assigned to the menu. Press Tab once so that 'Insert' is marked. Press Enter. The *Insert Macro Menu Item* window appears. Type the name of the macro, **ADDRESS** in the *Macro Name* box. If the macro is not located in the macro default directory, type the complete path in front of the macro name. Press Tab and in the *Menu Text* box type the text which is to be shown in the menu and which will allow you to recognize the macro. For example, *Name, address, phone*. Use Tab to move to *OK* and press Enter.

5.1.4   Removing macros from the menu

If you add macros to the menu now and again, it will eventually become full. If there are already nine macros in the menu, you will not be able to add a new one until you remove one of the others. How is this done?

M   Click on *Macro*, then *Assign to Menu*. Click on the menu text which belongs to the macro you wish to remove from the menu. Click on *Delete*.

K   Press Alt-M, then A. Using the cursor keys, highlight the text which belongs to the macro you wish to remove. Press Tab three times so that *Delete* is marked. Press Enter.

5.1.5   Additional possibilities

Assigning a macro to a button bar will be dealt with
later. For those who have some talent in computer programming, working with macros provides quite extensive possibilities. WPWin has its own 'Macro programming language' which, unfortunately (for technical
reasons) differs from the macro programming language
in WP 5.0 or WP 5.1 under DOS, so that macros created in other WP versions cannot easily be adopted into
WPWin. An extensive discussion concerning macro
language is not possible within the scope of this book.
WordPerfect has a separate manual dealing exclusively
with macros.

5.2   Screen display

The way in which things are shown on the screen can
be adjusted to suit your own requirements. A number of
possibilities are provided under *View* in the menu bar.
The Ruler will be discussed in chapter 7.

5.2.1   The Draft mode

Occasionally, the legibility of characters on the screen
can be unsatisfactory, especially if a small font has
been selected. As long as you are only busy typing the
text, you can make use of the *Concept* mode. You can
specify this as follows:

M   Click on *View*, then *Draft Mode*.

K   Press Alt-V, then D.

The text will then be displayed differently. The display
does not take the size and the shape of the letters into
account. If you wish to see (approximatetly) how it will
appear on paper, you must switch the concept mode off
in the same way as you switched it on.

5.2.2 Graphic images

If you wish to include graphic images in a document, it is very convenient to be able to see them immediately on the screen. However, this means that the formation of the screen display requires more time. If you wish to work a little quicker, switch off the graphics image display by removing the *Graphics* in the *View* menu. Select *View, Graphics* to do this. Repeating the procedure restores the tick mark.

5.2.3 Comments

If you wish to place some remarks in the text for your own use or for a colleague (comments which do not really belong to the text and are not going to be printed), proceed as follows:

M   Click on *Tools*, then *Comment*, then *Create*. A window appears in which you can type comments. In these comments, you may also use the bold, italics and underline features. When you have concluded the comments, click on *OK*.

K   Press Alt-T, then N, then C. A window appears in which you can type comments. In these comments, you may also use the bold, italics and underline features. When you have concluded the comments, press Enter.

The comments are shown on the screen on a grey background or in a rounded box. Using the menu options *Tools, Comment, Edit* or *Convert to Text*, you can alter the comments or convert to normal document text.

When you are busy with the layout of the document it is inconvenient to have the comments displayed on the screen. You will not be able to get a good impression of the final printed result. Accordingly, you can switch off the display of comments using the *View* menu. Select *View, Comments* and the display will be switched off. You can display it once more by repeating the process.

5.2.4   Short menus

If there are many functions which you do not regularly use in the menus, and this leads to time-consuming searching, you can try working with a shortened form of the drop-down menus.

For Short Menus to appear in the *View* menu, you must turn the Short Menus on. To do this, if this feature is not already active, insert the following lines in your WPWP.INI file:

```
[Settings]
EnableShortMenus=1
ShortMenus=1
```

'EnableShortMenus' when equal to 1, makes the Short Menus appear in the *View* menu.

'ShortMenus' when equal to 1, starts WPWin with Short Menus displayed.

M   Click on *View*, then *Short menus*. This shortens the menus.

K   Press Alt-V, then M. This shortens the menus.

If you prefer to work with the extended menus after all, repeat this procedure to restore the original options.

5.2.5   The status bar

The bar at the bottom of the screen is called the status bar. This shows, for instance, the position on paper of the letters being typed. The number of inches (or centimetres) from the top edge of the paper is shown (e.g. Ln 4" or 12.16 cm) as is the distance from the left edge of the paper (e.g. Pos 2" or 5.08 cm). You can display this position in inches, centimetres or in places, even in 1200ths of an inch. If you wish to change your settings, proceed as follows:

ℳ Click on *File, Preferences, Display*. The position display settings are shown in the status bar in the lower right-hand corner of the window. If you click on *inches* you will also see the other settings. Click on the required option. Click on *OK*.

𝒦 Press Alt-F, then E, then D. A window appears. Press Alt-B and by pressing the Cursor Up and Cursor Down keys you are able to see the various possibilities. When the appropriate option is marked press Enter.

As you will observe, there are many more settings which can be altered, but these concern details which we cannot deal with within the scope of this book. Of course, you may experiment with these settings. Each altered setting can easily be restored.

5.3   Codes in the 'Underwater screen'

A term well-known to experienced users of DOS versions of WordPerfect or LetterPerfect is the 'Display codes' function. A large amount of codes exist throughout the typed text, invisible to the user. These can be codes for bold, underlining etc, or codes for line and page layout such as alteration of margins or tabs, or codes for the specification of columns or tables, codes for hard returns, codes which specify hyphena-

tion etc. Especially in cases where settings are altered
later in the DOS versions of WordPerfect, it is important
to place the new settings precisely at the proper position and then remove the old codes. A window showing
the text along with all the applied codes can be activated by pressing Alt-F3.

In the Windows version of WordPerfect, placing codes
has been made somewhat easier. When you alter
something in the text format, the result is directly shown
on the screen. In addition, the correct codes are placed
at the proper position and any codes which have
become superfluous are removed. This expedites the
work and saves a great deal of searching and puzzling.

Nevertheless, it can be very useful to know which codes
are located where in the text. This can be done by looking at the 'underwater' screen:

m   Click on *View*, then *Reveal Codes*.

k   Press Alt-F3.

A part of your screen is now occupied by the 'underwater' screen. Using the cursor, you can move through
the screen and you will see simultaneously a cursor (in
the form of a red or dark block) moving through the
screen with codes. Just as you can delete characters on
the text screen one by one, you can also delete both
characters and codes in the same way on the 'underwater' screen.

To restore the normal text screen:

m   Click on *View*, then on *Reveal Codes*.

k   Press Alt-F3.

5.4   The button bar

A completely new and extremely useful function in WPWin is the button bar. This is a row of buttons on the screen which provides a number of well-used functions within easy reach. A **mouse** is essential for this.

5.4.1   Switching on and off

If you wish to switch on the button bar, click on *View* then *Button Bar*. Unless you have not installed any button bar files, the standard button bar will be shown.

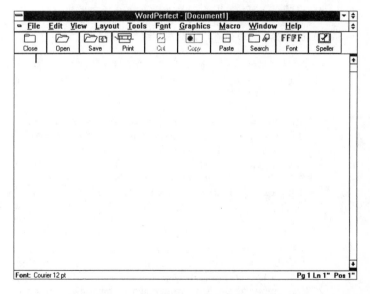

By clicking on one of the symbols on the button bar, you can select one of the following options quickly:

- Closing Files
- Opening files
- Saving files
- Printing
- Cutting (removing selected text)

- Copying selected text
- Pasting (inserting selected text)
- Speller
- Searching
- Font

In order to switch the button bar off again, click on *View*, then *Button Bar*.

5.4.2   Adding functions

In addition to the functions mentioned above, there are probably more functions which you regularly use. For instance, perhaps you often use italics or bold? How can italics be added to the button bar?

Select *View*, click on *Button Bar Setup*, click on *Edit*. A dialogue box will appear with a short outline of the procedure. Click on *Font* in the bar and then on *Italic*. A button for the italics function is added to the bar at the far right-hand side. It would be rather useful if the new button were situated immediately next to the Font option. This can be done. Click on the *Italics* button and drag it (holding down the left mouse button) to the left so that it partially overlaps the Font and Speller buttons. The *Italics* button will be inserted between Font and Speller.

If you often have to use characters which are not on the keyboard, you may find it useful to have a button for the WP character sets. Or perhaps you prefer to use the Ctrl-W key combination? If you do not wish to have to remember all the key combinations, create a button for the character sets.

(We presume that the *Edit Button Bar* box is still shown on your screen.) Click on *Font*, click on *WP Character Set*. A new button is added.

Meanwhile, the row of buttons has become so long that it no longer fits onto the screen. At the left-hand side, two small buttons have been added which allow you to shift the bar to the left and to the right. It is no longer particularly convenient. It would be advantageous to remove a feature you do not frequently use. Perhaps you don't really need *Print* since you do not use this feature much? We shall now remove *Print*. Click on the *Print* button, and drag it downwards. Release the mouse button when the *Print* button is outside the button bar. It will then disappear and the other buttons nestle in.

If you are satisfied with the new button bar arrangement, click on *OK*. Of course, you are free to alter as much as you wish.

5.4.3   Choosing another button bar

WPWin provides a choice of several button bars. How do you select another?

Click on *View*, then *Button Bar Setup*, then *Select*. A window will appear showing the names of three button bars. You have now worked with **wp{wp}.wwb**. There is an alternative button bar, **features.wwb** and also one which has been formulated to create and edit tables or worksheets, **tables.wwb**. Click on **second.wwb** and click on *Select*. A button bar with completely different functions will appear for editing text and recording and running macros.

5.4.4   Moving the button bar

On a normal 14 inch computer screen not a great deal of text can be seen, but if a button bar is also situated along the top the number of lines visible becomes even smaller. There are two solutions to this problem: Only show the text instead of showing buttons with pictures and text, or move the button bar to the left or right-hand side of the screen. If you do both, you will have room for many more buttons!

Click on *View*, *Button Bar Setup* and *Options*. In the
Button Bar Options box, click on *Left*, on *Text Only* and
on *OK*. Observe the result. More space has been made
available for text on the screen and due to the reduced
size there is more room for adding new functions to the
button bar.

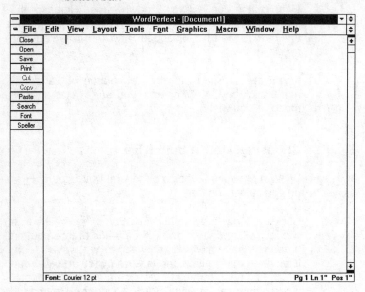

5.4.5   New button bar

You can easily create a new button bar containing functions geared to your own requirements. Click on *View*,
Button Bar Setup, New. Now select the menu options
you wish to have in your button bar. New buttons are
made automatically. Click on *OK*. The *Save Button Bar*
dialogue box appears on the screen. Enter the name
you wish to assign to the button bar and click on *Save*.

5.4.6   Adding a macro to the button bar

You can add the macros which you have created yourself to the button bar. As practice, we shall use the
macro YOURS which we made in section 5.1.1 to conclude a letter. Click on *View*, *Button Bar Setup* and *Edit*.
Click on *Assign Macro to Button Bar*. A list of macros
will appear. Click on the required macro name and click
on *Assign*. Click on *OK*. The button bar has now been
enriched with a self-made macro.

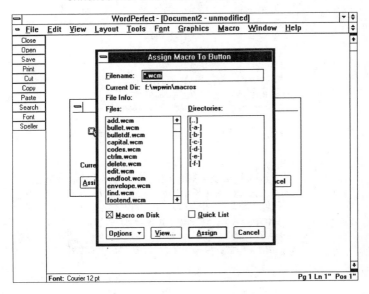

Exercises

1. Make a new button bar which provides the func-
    tions Retrieve, Save, Close, Bold, Italics, Normal,
    Speller, and Create Comment. Assign the name
    SELFMADE to the button bar.

2. Remove the Comment function from the button bar
    and add Font. Place the button bar at the left-hand
    side of the screen.

3.   Make a macro to select one word. Call it WORD-SEL. Add the macro to the SELFMADE button bar.

Procedures

1.   Click on *View*, then *Button Bar Setup, New.* Select the required functions by clicking on the appropriate menu options listed below:

Retrieve: *File, Retrieve*
Save: *File, Save*
Close: *File, Close*
Bold: *Font, Bold*
Italics: *Font, Italic*
Normal: *Font, Normal*
Speller: *Tools, Speller*
Comment: *Tools, Comment, Create*

Click on *OK*, enter the name SELFMADE, click on *Save*.

2.   Ensure that the SELFMADE button bar is displayed on the screen. Click on *View, Button Bar Setup, Edit.* Click on the *Comment* button, drag it into the text box and release the mouse button. Click on *Font, Font.* Click on *OK*. Click on *View, Button Bar Setup, Options.* Click on *Left*, then on *OK*.

3.   Ensure that the SELFMADE button bar is displayed on the screen. Place the cursor at the beginning of any word. Click on *Macro, Record.* Enter WORD-SEL. Click in the *Descriptive Name* box and enter: select one word. Click on *Record.* Hold down the Shift key while pressing Ctrl-Cursor Right to select a word. Now exactly one word has been selected. Click on *Macro*, then on *Stop.* Click in the text to undo the selection. Click on *View, Button Bar Setup, Edit, Assign Macro to Button Bar.* Double click on *wordsel.wcm.* Click on *OK*.

6   Selecting fonts

A font is a complete range of letters and numbers shar-
ing similar graphical features. Each font has its own
style. Related fonts (for example the Roman, italics,
bold and bold italic of the same basic font) form font
families. It is usually possible to print texts in various
fonts on most printers. In addition, Windows provides a
number of alternative fonts for most printers.

6.1   Printer drivers: WordPerfect or Windows?

The fonts you use depend upon the possibilities provided by your printer and the printer driver you have
chosen. Windows requires a special printer driver and
supplies a number of fonts for use, regardless of the
chosen printer. In addition, the internal printer fonts can
also be used.

Nevertheless, you can also use the WordPerfect 5.1
printer driver when working with WPWin. This also
allows you to print foreign fonts and graphical characters not made available by most printers. WordPerfect
offers the choice between usage of its own, or of the
Windows printer driver. The advantages and disadvan-
tages of these will be further discussed in chapters 14
and 15.

6.2   Fonts with and without serif

For centuries it was the custom to use all kinds of
strokes, curls and embellishments on written letters.
Printed letters were usually a bit simpler, but they were
still often adorned with little horizontal or vertical lines,
called *serif*. It became customary only in the course of
the twentieth century to use letters without *serif* for
printed matter and correspondence. The diagrams

below display examples of fonts with and without serif (sans serif).

Times Roman

New Century Schoolbook

Garamond

Bookman

The most common fonts with serif which occur on printers are:

- Times Roman, also referred to as Times or Roman, which is the classical newspaper font. Variants exist under the names Dutch, Nimbus Roman and BR- TMS.
- Courier (with the variants Brougham and Nimbus Mono) which strongly resembles the font on a typewriter or computer screen (in non-graphic programs). This is the default font in all printers, in other words, if you do not specify another font the text will be printed using the Courier font.
- New Century Schoolbook, with the Century Schoolbook variant. This is a font which was developed in the US in 1915 for school books and is commonly recognized as being an easily-read font.
- Garamond, which is a little more elegant than the previous font, but is also easily-read.
- Palatino, which is more ornate than the previously mentioned types, originating in ancient Italy. It is also known as Zapf Calligraphic, with a variant under the name Palermo.
- Bookman, also known as ITC Bokkman or Revival, which is a rather conservative, business-like, neutral font which is easily read.
- Berkeley, a font with a classical appearance, which makes a distinguished impression.

The most common fonts without serif are:

- Helvetica, with the variants Swiss 721, Arial, Nimbus Sans and BR-HLV. This is a widely-used print font, a little less formal than other fonts without serif.
- Sans Serif, a taut, simple font.
- Futura, a rigid, almost bare font. The strictly vertical lines and the circular O are particularly striking.
- Avant Garde, also called Geometric, which is a little broader and rounder than Helvetica.
- Univers, which resembles these four to a certain extent.
- Helvetica Narrow or Helvetica Condensed and Swiss 712 or Nimbus Sans Narrow, a smaller version of the Helvetica font. This requires getting used to, but is certainly not illegible. More letters fit onto one line.
- Modern, a slim Window font. (There is also a Modern font with serif.)
- Frutiger, a rigid but not inelegant font.

Helvetica

Futura

Avant Garde

Univers Light

6.3   Bold and italics

In addition to the normal version of fonts, there are generally also **bold** and *italic* versions. These are chiefly supplied as separate fonts on the printer. In the Font list **bold** is sometimes also called **heavy** and *italic* also called *oblique*. If the font provides the bold and italic variants, it will usually also supply the ***bold italic*** or ***bold oblique*** version too.

In order to print sections of text in bold or italics, it is not necessary to select the relevant font. Entering a code for bold or italic is sufficient.

6.4   Proportional fonts

Not all letters are equally wide. An **i** or an **l** is considerably thinner than an **m** or a **w**. On a typewriter, each letter must occupy the same amount of space. Then we refer to a *fixed character width*. In fact, the **m** becomes too narrow and the i is made artificially wide by means of serif. This is also the case in the Courier font, which is the default font on most printers, i.e. the font used for printing unless another font is specified. Courier is also the font required by bookkeeping programs in order to print sums precisely underneath one another.

Most other fonts are proportional, which means that thin letters occupy less space than their broader counterparts. Usage of proportional fonts is preferable in correspondence, essays, books etc. When working with proportional fonts, the great advantage of the Windows version of WordPerfect becomes obvious: you are able to see on the screen exactly how the printer will distribute the letters on the paper.

6.5   Font size

The size of a font is mainly expressed in *points* and occasionally in *cpi (characters per inch)*. The size in points refers to the height of the letter: the more points, the taller the letter. There are 72 points to an inch.

Normally, 10, 11 or 12 point size is used for correspondence. Larger is unnecessary and smaller becomes difficult to read. Nevertheless, smaller letters are used in newspapers, dictionaries, encyclopedias and other printed matter, not to mention the 'small print' in contracts and policies!

The font size referred to in *cpi (characters per inch)* indicates the letter width, expressed as a fraction of an inch. With a font size of 10 cpi, each letter is a tenth of an inch wide. The rule is: the greater the number, the smaller the letter. The letter size can vary from 5 to 16.66 cpi.

Since the term *cpi* entails that each letter receives the same amount of space, this is only used for fonts with a fixed character width. In the case of a proportional font, not every letter needs to be equally wide.

Fonts with a fixed character width can be distinguished from **scalable fonts**. Matrix printers and inkjet printers generally have a number of fonts which are available in one size or in sizes which vary very little. Laser printers frequently have scalable fonts available, in which you can adjust the size of the font without limit, for example from 5 points to 500. (A 500 point letter will fill a whole page on its own!)

Examples of different font sizes:

Helvetica (8 points)
Helvetica (10 points)
Helvetica (12 points)
Helvetica (14 points)
Helvetica (18 points)
Helvetica (24 points)

6.6   Which font?

First impressions of a printed document are often determined to an important extent by the font used. The legibility is also dependent upon this.

The desired impression is also linked to the associations evoked by a certain font.

- A rigid letter, such as most fonts without serif, tends to make a business-like impression. A neutral font, such as Bookman, may also give this impression.
- An elegant font, such as those with serif, tend to make a more personal impression.
- In modern situations, for instance in the fields of electronics, air travel or automatisation, a rigid font is preferable. Use Univers and Futura. If your printer does not supply this kind of font, consider using the Windows printer driver which does enable you to use the Modern Windows font.
- The reader associates soundness and reliability with a classical font. A solicitor or lawyers' office or the director of a large company may consider use of Times, Roman, (New) Century Schoolbook, Garamond, Bookman and Berkely or even Helvetica, the most classical of the fonts without serif.
- Anyone who sells classical furniture or clothes, or antiques or other traditional products may wish to emphasize the proven values by selecting a traditional font. Consider Times/Roman, Garamond and Palatino, or Berkely for antique or traditional products.
- Posters or programmes for classical music, theatre or ballet tend to do well if a traditional, elegant font is used. Garamond, Palatino and Berkely are obvious choices, but Times (Roman), (New) Century Schoolbook or even Helvetica or Frutiger may also be kept in mind.
- For modern music, theatre and dance and jazz a more contemporary font should be chosen. Avant Garde (what's in a name?), Futura, Univers and Sans Serif are serious candidates. Helvetica, Frutiger and Bookman are a little more neutral.
- Use of uncommon fonts can assist in eye-catching presentation, but this is not advisable in serious business correspondence.

If a company wishes to be taken notice of, it should present itself in a **characteristic style**. On the other hand, if topics which differ radically according to subject matter have to be presented, a choice should be made for a standard font which satisfies the majority of requirements.

Regardless of what you write and to whom, pay attention to the legibility. In English and American publications about desktop publishing, we often encounter lengthy sections of text in a font without serif which are not pleasant to read. For this reason, in Great Britain and North America, Garamond, Century Schoolbook or Bookman are most frequently used, along with the more modern fonts Futura, Univers or Frutiger. Helvetica (used for this book) seldom gives rise to difficulties.

Keep in mind:

■ A text containing many numbers or special characters occasionally causes problems. There are fonts in which the small letter L and the number one strongly resemble one another, or in which the small letter L cannot be distinguished from a vertical stripe.

■ Lengthy sections of text which are printed in an unusual font (ornate letters, fantasy letters) often substantially decrease the legibility.

■ Some fonts provide only capitals. An entire paragraph printed in capitals is very laborious for the reader. A whole page may only work preventatively. This kind of font should only be used for headings.

6.7 Combining fonts

Combining different fonts in one document may produce pleasing results but it can also be risky. If there are (too) many fonts, this will tend to give a rather chaotic impression.

In letters etc. it is best to stick to one font. If you do not use headed paper, you may use an alternative font for your own name and address if it is placed at the top or at the bottom of the letter.

In folders, brochures or other printed matter dealing with presentation, you may emphasize certain sections of text by placing it in another font. However, a continual switch back and forth between two fonts is very tedious.

In a case like this, it is better to choose two variants of
the same font, for instance normal and italics, or 11
point size and 14. It's not a bad idea to assign a different
font to headings. You can employ an ornate or otherwise noticeable font for these. A combination which you
will often encounter in software manuals is Helvetica
Bold (thus a bold font without serif) for the headings,
and New Century Schoolbook (a normal font with serif)
for the paragraphs. Other combinations are also very
acceptable.

6.8   Specifying fonts

Three factors determine the fonts you use:

- the printer you use,
- the printer driver you use, the WordPerfect driver or
  the Windows driver,
- use of extra fonts from utility programs while printing.

Each printer provides a certain amount of built-in fonts.
This quantity may vary from two or three to more than
thirty. The printer driver in WordPerfect allows you to
make optimal use of these fonts, at the same time providing the possibility of printing special characters with
which the printer itself is not familiar. On the other hand,
the Windows printer driver makes available a number of
standard Windows fonts which can always be printed,
regardless of the type of printer. Printing these special
Windows fonts does take place a little slower. This topic
is discussed more extensively in chapter 15.

WPWin distinguishes between three sorts of fonts:

- The basic printer font. This is the font which is automatically selected as soon as you select a certain
  printer. If you do not select a font for a document,
  WPWin prints your text in the basic font for the selected printer type.
- The initial document font. This can always be specified while working on a document. From the position

where you choose the initial font onwards, this font is used, except where you temporarily use another type. Bold and italics can normally be regarded as temporary variants of an initial font.
■ Temporary fonts. You can select a block of text and assign special features to it (bold, small, extra large etc.) or even select a complete other font for it (Courier instead of Roman, for instance). At the end of the selected block, the font most recently selected as the initial font will be restored.

6.9   Changing the default font for the printer

If you alter the default font for the printer, the newly specified font is automatically chosen for each new document which is linked to this printer.
Another font is only used when you specially determine it for a particular document. Select the font you most prefer to use as default font for the printer. This will save you the work of specifying an initial font for a great number of documents.

Changing the default font for the printer is done as follows:

m   Click on *File*, then *Select Printer*, then *Setup*. Click on *Initial Font*. The *Printer Initial Font* window will appear. You will see a list of fonts. Using the scroll bars, you can browse through all the fonts available. If you click on a font name, it will be displayed in the broad text box. When you have found the font you require, click on *OK*. Click on *OK* once again, then on *Close*.

к   Press Alt-F, then L. Press Alt-E, then Alt-F. The Printer Initial Font window will appear. Using the Cursor Up and Cursor Down keys, you can browse through the fonts. An example of each font is displayed in the broad text window. Press Enter when the required font is highlighted. Press Enter once more and then Alt-F4.

𝒟   Proceed as above, but press F7 to conclude.

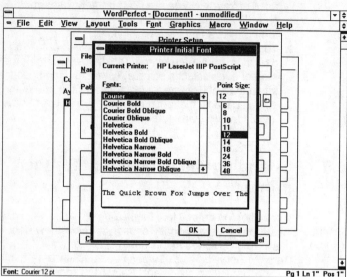

6.10   Changing the document initial font

If you are satisfied with the default printer font, you do
not have to specify this initial font for every new document: WPWin will do this automatically. In addition, it is
possible to choose a different initial font while working
on a document. This is then applied from the current
cursor position onwards until the end of the document,
or until you again specify a different font.

If you wish to specify an initial font for one entire document, this should be done at the beginning of the document. Proceed as follows:

𝓜   Click on *Font*, then on *Font*. Click on one of the fonts in
the left-hand window. An example of this font will be
shown in the box underneath. Double click on the font,
or on *OK*.

K   Press F9. Or press Alt-O, then O. Using Cursor Up or Cursor Down, you can select the required font. Press Enter.

D   Press Ctrl-F8. Select the required font and press Enter.

If you use the Ruler (this will be dealt with in chapter 7), you can also proceed as follows:

M   Click on *Font*. Select one of the fonts available.

If you decide to change the font in a document, this can done for the entire document including headers and footers, regardless of the current insertion point:

M   Select *Layout*, *Document*, and then *Initial Font*. The Document Initial Font dialogue box appears. Select the required font and click on *OK*.

K   Press Alt-L, D and then F. The Initial Font dialogue box appears. Highlight the required font and press Enter.

6.11   Changing font temporarily

You may choose a different font for a single sentence or line or paragraph if you wish. First mark the text to which you wish to assign the deviating font. When this has been done, proceed just as you would do when specifying an initial document font. The difference is that the newly specified font only applies to the selected block of text. Subsequently, the most recently specified initial font is reinstated.

6.12   Changing the display

In many cases, you can retain the same initial font and only alter the display. Mark a block of text and proceed as follows:

M   Click on *Font*, then select *Bold, Italic* or *Underline*.

𝒦   If you wish to select Bold Italic or Underline, press respectively Ctrl-B, Ctrl-I or Ctrl-U. Otherwise, press Alt-O, then B, I or U.

𝒟   You can use F6 or Ctrl-B for Bold, F8 or Ctrl-U for Underline and Ctrl-I for Italics. Otherwise, press Alt-O and then B, I or U.

6.13   Changing font size

In some cases, you may wish to retain the same initial font but wish to use a larger or smaller version. Keep in mind that not all printers are capable of printing all fonts larger or smaller. Specifying a larger or smaller letter is done as follows:

𝓜   Click on *Font*, then *Size*, then select *Fine, Small, Large, Very Large* or *Extra Large*.

𝒦   Press Alt-O, then S. Then select F, S, L V or E, as you require.

Exercises

1.   Retrieve the REPORT file. Select a different font for the entire document. Choose a larger font size for the heading. Save the modified document under the name REPORT2 and clear the screen.

2.   Retrieve the GLASS document. Now make the heading bold and change the personal names to italics. Have the title no longer centred but place it two tab stops from the left margin. Save the document under the name GLASS2 and clear the screen.

Procedures

1. Select *File, Retrieve*. Select **report**. Ensure that the
    cursor is located at the beginning of the text. Click
    on *Font, Font*. Examine the available fonts by using
    Cursor Up or Cursor Down or by clicking on the
    scroll arrows. Select a pleasant but simple font,
    Century Schoolbook, Helvetica or Univers for in-
    stance. When the corresponding font is highlighted,
    press Enter.
    Place the cursor on the first line at the beginning of
    the word 'Mist'. Mark the heading by holding down
    the Shift key and pressing End. Click on *Font, Size,
    Large*. If your printer is not able to print a larger font
    size, WordPerfect will attempt to emphasize the
    text in another way, such as bold or underlining.
    Examine the specified codes using Alt-F3. The
    codes are indeed registered, [Large on] and [Large
    off].
    Click on *File, Save As*. Assign the name **report2**
    and press Enter. Click on *File, Close*.

2. Select *File, Retrieve*. Press Alt-I to move to the
    Files box and, using the Cursor Down key, highlight
    the required file name. Press Enter. Ensure that the
    cursor is located at the beginning of the text. Mark
    the heading by holding down Shift and pressing
    End. Select *Font, Bold*.
    Place the cursor in front of the first letter of the word
    Charlton and mark the name by holding down Shift
    and pressing the Cursor Right key. Then press Ctrl-
    I. Do the same for the other names.
    Press Alt-F3 to check the codes. Place the cursor
    on the code [Just:Centre] so that this changes col-
    our or shading. Press Del. Press Tab twice.
    Press Alt-F to select *File*, then A to select *Save As*.
    Type the name **glass2** and press Enter. Press Alt-
    F and type C.

7   Adjusting line and page layout

7.1   Line format

There are a great number of possibilities for adjusting the line spacing. They are all approached in the same way:

M   Click on *Layout*, then *Line*. Subsequently click on one of the items in the submenu.

K   Press Shift-F9, then type one of the underlined letters in the submenu. Instead of Shift-F9, you can press Alt-L, then L.

D   Press Shift-F8 (or Alt-L), then press L, then select one of the underlined letters in the submenu.

7.1.2   Setting tabs

You can place tabs with a precision of a sixteenth of an inch. This is done in the Position box of the Tab Set window. For each individual tab you can make a choice between:

■ Left Align: this is the 'normal' tab, as it appears on the typewriter. The tab is set at a fixed place and all typed text is entered to the right of the tab.
■ Centre: equal amounts of text are placed to the left and right of the tab.
■ Right Align: only the right side is fixed, all text is placed to the left of the tab.
■ Decimal Align: a fixed character (for example, a comma, a point or a dash) is placed at the tab point, the other characters entered are placed to the right and left of that character.
■ Dot leader: this feature can be combined with other options. Points (dots) are placed between the text at the tab and the previous text.

When you have typed the required position and have specified the relevant options, click on *Set Tab*. This dialogue box can also be used to delete tabs, either individually or collectively. By clicking on *Default* the default tab setting is restored.

7.1.3 Absolute and relative tabs

WordPerfect works with absolute and relative tabs. If you select absolute tabs, the distance is calculated from the left edge of the paper. If you select relative tabs, the distance is calculated from the left margin.

As the left margin is altered, all tabs move with it. This is the default setting in WordPerfect. If you wish to change this, go to the Tab Set window and activate the *Left Edge* option in the *Position From* box.

7.1.4 Line spacing

The line spacing is the room *between* the lines. The default setting is 1, but this can be varied without limit. A spacing just a little larger (1.1 or 1.2) can increase the legibility in many cases, and a fraction smaller (0.9 will help in getting more lines onto a page in cases of emergency. Drastically reducing the line spacing is not recommended. Setting the line spacing is self-explanatory. The setting applies *from* the point in the text where you made the change, onwards. If you wish to alter the line spacing in the entire document, first place the cursor at the beginning of the text.

7.1.5 Line height

The line height consists of the letter height plus blank space. The line height is automatically adjusted by WordPerfect to each font, but you may also specify a fixed line height, independent of the font. When you have activated the *Line Height* dialogue box, click on either *Auto* or *Fixed*. You can also make a selection by pressing either Alt-A or Alt-F. If you select *Fixed*, you can specify a height yourself. WordPerfect automatically enters the number which applies to the specified font.

7.1.6   Line numbering

You can number the lines and, in doing so, specify whether all lines should be preceded by a number or only, for instance, every fifth or tenth line. In addition, you can specify the starting number and whether blank lines should be counted or not. You can number the lines according to each page or cumulatively for the entire document. Line numeration is not displayed on the screen unless you request a print preview (see chapter 14).

7.2   Pagination (hard page break)

When you have typed text for a document and you are looking through it, you will observe that it repeatedly occurs that a new page begins right in the middle of a paragraph, just before or after a new topic, or at another unfortunate place. By placing the cursor at a certain point in the text and pressing Ctrl-Enter, you can indicate that a new page *must* begin here. The code which is then placed in the text is called *Hard page break [HPg]*.

7.3   Widows and orphans

One way of preventing an unfortunate division of paragraphs is to activate the *Widow/Orphan* protection. This refers to single lines of a paragraph being placed at the top or bottom of a page while the rest of the paragraph is placed on another page. Setting this protection takes place using *Layout, Page, Widow/Orphan*.

7.4   Vertically centring the text

The text can also be vertically centred using the *Layout, Page* menu. If there is insufficient text to fill a whole page, the text is placed in such a way that there are equal amounts of blank space above and below the text. If you wish the blank space below the text to be a little larger than that above, you should press Enter several times to create blank lines. These blank lines are counted in the centring process.

7.5   Page numbering

You can have the pages of your document numbered when they are printed. This can be very useful, certainly with lengthy documents. Select *Numbering* in the *Layout, Page* menu. The *Page Numbering* dialogue box will appear.

In the 'Position' text box, mark *No Page Numbering* by pressing Tab several times, or by clicking on it using the mouse. By pressing Cursor Down, various methods of setting page numbers will be shown. If you are going to print double-sided, you can place the page numbering alternately right and left, top or bottom.
The *Numbering Type* box allows you to select either Arabic or Roman numbers, the latter in capital or small letters.

If you place the page numbering in headers or footers, a code must be entered for this. The standard code is ^B (created by pressing Ctrl+B simultaneously). If you wish to use a different code, specify it in the the *Accompanying Text* box.

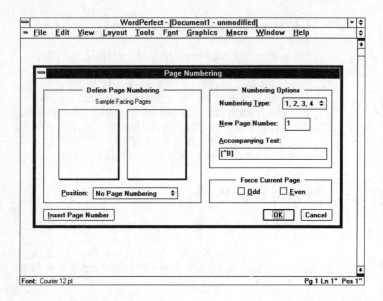

7.6   Headers and footers

If you create a text which is several pages long, it can be useful to place a header above the text, in order to indicate the origin of the text and/or the topic it is dealing with. If you wish, you can also include a page number in the header or footer.

A header or footer need not be confined to a single line, it may occupy several lines. Graphic elements may also be included in the header. Do not forget to specify the font you wish to have in the header or footer. If you are working with left- and right-hand pages, you may wish to have differing headers or footers. This provides the possibility of placing more information in the header or footer without that costing more space on each page. For instance, you can display the title of a book on the left page and the name of the chapter in the header on the right-hand page. In addition, for the symmetry, you could place the page numbers alternately at the left and right at the top of the pages.

Instead of headers, you can use footers. These are created in exactly the same way, only select *footer* instead of *header* in the *Layout, Page* menu.

Headers and footers can both be used at the same time. Accordingly, you can place the title and the date in the header of a report or bulletin, for example, and the company name or department in the footer.

Finally, it can be extremely useful to work with footers if you have a document of only one page and you wish to have one or several lines completely at the bottom. Then it is not necessary to measure the page length. Specify the appropriate lines as being a footer and they will be automatically placed at the bottom.

In order to create a header which is repeated on each page, proceed as follows:

Select *Layout, Page, Header*. Select *Header A* if there is no other header. Click on *Create* or press Enter. You can now type the header. If you wish to include a page number, click on *Page Number* (or press Alt-N) when the cursor is at the required position. The code will be placed automatically. Using the *Placement* option, you can specify whether the header should be printed on every page or on odd or even pages. If you create two headers, you can place them alternately on the left- or right-hand pages. Select on *Close* (Alt-C) when the header is complete.

Creating a footer occurs in exactly the same way. The only difference is that it is placed at the bottom of the page. If you select *Edit* header or footer, WordPerfect automatically displays the corresponding text.

Caution: headers and footers which are not specified at the beginning of a document will not be printed on all pages.

7.7   Suppressing page numbers, headers and footers

It is not always desirable to print page numbers, headers or footers on every page. It is sometimes better to omit them, particularly on the first or last page. On pages with large pictures or diagrams, it is also better to exclude them. Using the *Layout, Page* menu, go to the *Suppress* dialogue box. This allows you to specify what you do not wish to have on a certain page: header or footer or page number. If required, you can also place a page number at the Bottom Centre, regardless of the normal position of the page number.

7.8   Column sort

WordPerfect distinguishes between two sorts of columns: newspaper style and parallel. Columns in newspaper style cover the whole length of the page and lend themselves for long, continuous articles. When the first column is full, the text continues at the top of the second column. Parallel columns contain texts which must be placed next to one another. The texts begin equally at the start of each new paragraph.

7.8.1   Column definition

Before placing text in columns, you must first define the columns. Select *Layout, Columns, Define*. The *Define Columns* dialogue box appears. Normally, the WordPerfect default setting is two columns, equally wide, in newspaper style, with a space of half an inch between the columns. Using the mouse or the Tab key, you can move through the options in this box and change the settings as required. The maximum amount of columns is 24, but on a normal page, it is not advisable to have more than three or four columns, otherwise a very small font will be needed. If you alter the spacing between the columns, the left and right margins will be automatically adjusted. If you do not wish the columns to be equally wide, you must specify exactly where you wish to have the margins for each column.

You may choose between Newspaper, Parallel or Parallel Block Protect. If you select this last option, you will avoid sections of text which belong together being divided over different pages. If there is a cross next to *Columns On*, all subsequent text will be set in columns from the position at which you made the column definition.

An example of columns in newspaper style:

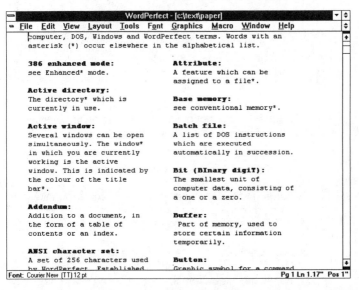

If you are working with parallel columns, you can force a shift to another column by pressing Ctrl-Enter, even when you are not at the bottom of the page. If you do not wish to place the remainder of the text in columns, select *Layout, Columns*, go to the Options box and ensure that there is no cross in the Columns On box.

An example of parallel columns:

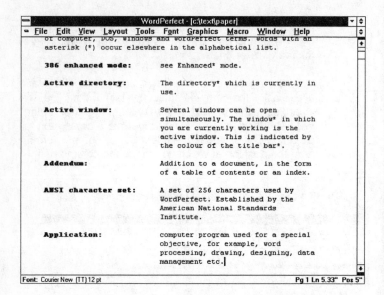

If you have chosen block protection, and a line of a paragraph does not fit into the corresponding page, the whole block will shift to the following page.

7.8.2   Moving the cursor in columns

In order to return to another column, you can make use of the key combination listed below:

Alt-Cursor Right: move to the same line in the column to the right;

Alt-Cursor Left: move to the same line in the column to the left.

The mouse allows you to choose a new position quickly and easily.

7.9   The Ruler

Various formatting functions in WPWin can be implemented rapidly using the mouse and the Ruler. The Ruler can be displayed by clicking on *View* then *Ruler* or by pressing Alt-Shift-F3.

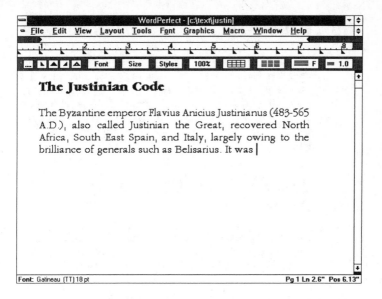

The actual Ruler, showing inches, indicates the width of the paper. Various sorts of triangles represent various sorts of tabs. You can remove a tab by dragging it out of the Ruler. A new tab can be set by grabbing a tab at the left in the grey bar and dragging it to the required position on the Ruler.

If you wish to create tabs with dot leaders, click on the button at the extreme left of the grey bar. Click once more and the tabs no longer have dot leaders.

Using the menu *Font, Font* and the *Assign to Ruler* option, you can place fonts in a new Ruler drop-down menu. In addition, the Ruler contains buttons for Fonts, Size, Styles, Tables, Columns, Justification and Spacing options.
These are activated by clicking on the required icon, highlighting the required option and double clicking or pressing Enter.

7.10   Setting columns using the Ruler

Setting columns is quite simple. Select the number of
columns (only newspaper style is possible here). Shift
the small block with the arrows which is just above the
Ruler if you wish unequal columns. This indicates
where the columns begin. If you wish to discontinue
working in columns, select *Columns Off* using the
Ruler.

7.11   Justification options using the Ruler

Using the *Justification options* menu, you can choose
whether you wish to have the text left- or right-aligned,
centred or totally justified (left- and right-aligned).

7.12   Line spacing using the Ruler

The last menu enables you to quickly adjust the line
spacing to 1.0, 1.5 or 2.0. If you wish to have other
values, you must do that using the *Layout* menu.

Styles and Tables will be discussed later.

7.13   Assigning fonts to the Ruler

You can use the Ruler to specify fonts, but these must
be assigned to the Ruler first. That is done as follows:

M   Click on *Font*, then *Font*. The *Font* dialogue box will ap-
           pear. Click on *Assign to Ruler*. In the list of fonts, click on
           the font you wish to assign. If this is not visible, use the
           scroll bar buttons to draw it into the box. Click twice on
           OK.

K   Press F9, or first Alt-O, then O. The *Font* dialogue box
           will appear. Press Alt-A. Using the Cursor Down key,

move through the fonts until the required font is highlighted. Then press Alt-A. Press Enter, then Esc.

𝒟   Press Ctrl-F8, or first Alt-O and then O. Press Alt-A and
using Cursor Down, move through the font list until the
required font is highlighted. Press Alt-A, then Enter,
then F1.

7.14   Specifying fonts using the Ruler

Specifying a font using the Ruler is extremely easy. Ensure that the cursor is at the position where the new font
should come. Click on *Font* and release the mouse button when the required font is highlighted. Check
whether it has actually been selected.

Exercises

1.   Begin a new document. Place the title at the top:
Two Reports. Leave two lines blank and retrieve
the REPORT file. Leave two lines blank under this
document and then retrieve the GLASS document.
Now specify new margins: top, left and right 2", bottom 5". Specify the line spacing as 1.4. Number the
pages in the lower right-hand corner. Save this document as TWINREP and clear the screen.

2.   Retrieve TWINREP. Specify the left and right margins at 1.5". Place the text in columns from "Thick"
onwards in newspaper style. Save the document
as TWINREP2 and clear the screen.

Procedures

1.   Type the title. Press Enter three times. Select *File,
Retrieve*. Select **report**. Move the cursor to the end
and press Enter three times. Retrieve **glass** in the
same way. Place the cursor at the beginning of the
text and select *Layout, Margins*. Change the mar-

gins to 2, 2, 2 and 5 (move to each new category by
clicking on it or by pressing Tab). Press Enter.
Select *Layout, Line, Spacing*. Change the line
spacing to 1.4 and press Enter.
Select *Layout, Page, Numbering*. Go to the *Posi-
tion* box and move through the options until *Bottom
Right* is marked. Press Enter.
Select *File*, then *Save As*. Specify the name TWIN-
REP and press Enter. Select *File, Close*.

2.   Select *File, Retrieve*. Select **twinrep**. Ensure that
the cursor is positioned at the beginning of the text.
Select *Layout, Margins*. Alter the left and right mar-
gins to 1.5" and press Enter.
Place the cursor just in front of the T of Thick. Se-
lect *Layout, Columns, Define*. Move to the *Distance
Between Columns* box and change 0.5 to 0.75.
Press Enter.
Select *File, Save As*. Specify TWINREP2. Select
File, Close.

8 Graphics

You cannot make any drawings or pictures using Word-Perfect, but you can adopt illustrations into the text. Drawings can be used which have been created using DrawPerfect or the graphic program Paintbrush which is supplied along with Windows. (Do not confuse Paintbrush with PC Paintbrush which is a much more extensive program.) In addition, a whole range of graphic files is supplied along with WordPerfect. These can be recognized by the .WPG extension, and can be adopted, ready-made, into your documents.

8.1 Making a figure box

Before adopting an image into text, you must specify where it is to be situated. Place the cursor at the appropriate position. Now select *Graphics, Figure, Retrieve* or press F11. The names of the pictures in the WPWin Graphics subdirectory are shown. You can activate one of these images or an image which has been made using a graphic program and which is stored in another directory. Before deciding to use a graphic file, you can look into it first.

8.2 Working with an image

When you activate an image, it is automatically placed in a frame at the right-hand side of the page. Perhaps this is not really what you had in mind. By clicking on the image using the **right** mouse button, a menu with three options will be displayed on the screen. Choose *Edit Figure*.

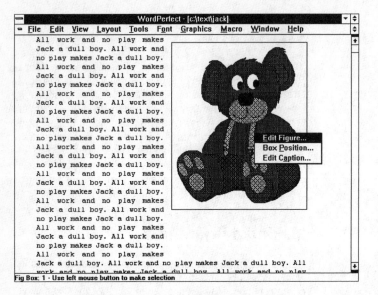

Fig Box: 1 - Use left mouse button to make selection

You now enter a large window, the *Figure Editor*. The corresponding button bar is at the left of the screen. This provides the following possibilities:

- Close: do this when you have completed the edit.
- Retrieve: use this to activate a drawing.
- Fig Pos: use this to locate the figure box where you want it on the page.
- Move: use this to move the figure within the box.
- Rotate: use this to rotate the figure. The rotation steps are shown in degrees in the lower right-hand corner of the screen.
- Enlarge: by specifying an area of the image, you can enlarge it to fill the screen. Hold down the left mouse button and define the area you wish to enlarge by dragging a rectangle over the relevant area.
- Reset Size: restores the image to the original size.
- Mirror: Mirrors the image.
- Outline: removes colour or other packing so that only black lines remain. This is a useful feature if you have a printer which cannot print colours or grey areas.

- Reset All: restores the original state. All alterations are undone.
- Edit All: enables you to enlarge the image horizontally or vertically or both, to specify accurately how much it should be moved, to specify the degree of rotation, to display in monochrome, to display in inverse video (light becomes dark, vice versa, or colours are replaced by their complements).

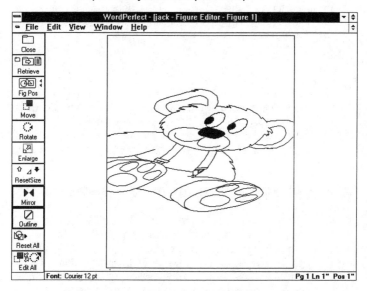

When you have concluded working on the figure, click on *Close*.

8.3   Moving the image

In your document, you can also move the image on the screen (and thus also on the paper) without having to make use of a menu. Using the left mouse button, click on any position inside the frame of the image. The mouse pointer changes into a four-pointed star.

Now, holding down the left mouse button, you are able

to move the figure in any direction. If you move the
pointer to a corner of the frame, it changes into a
double-arrow. You can now alter the format (and form!)
of the image frame. When you are satisfied with the position of the figure, click once anywhere outside the
image frame and it will be anchored there.

You can also relocate the figure or change the format by
clicking on the figure using the right mouse button and
then selecting an option from the *Box Position and Size*
menu which then appears.

8.4   Captions

By clicking on a figure with the right-hand mouse button
and then choosing *Edit Caption*, you are able to provide
illustrations with a caption. In the same way, you can
later alter a caption which has been created in this way.

8.5   Images from other programs

There are a great many more possibilities to illustrate
your texts than are supplied free with WordPerfect.
Each program with which you can create BMP-, CGM-,
DHP-, DXF-, EPS-, GEM-, HPGL-, IMG-, MSP-, PCX-,
PIC-, PNTG-, PPIC-, TIFF-, WMF- or WPG files can be
used to provide images for WordPerfect for Windows.

Many programs are capable of saving a created or
edited image in various formats. You should select a
format which WordPerfect is able to handle. If you wish
to use files made using WPWin, to which illustrations
have been added, in the DOS version of WordPerfect
5.1, keep in mind that it will not support all the file formats mentioned above. Consult the WP 5.1 for DOS
manual about this. Some files must first be converted to
another format using a WP conversion program.

Below, there is a concise survey of how to apply images
created using other programs in WPWin.

8.5.1   Images from PlanPerfect

Create the image. When the image is on the screen, select Save (F10) and save it as .WPG image. If you wish
to use the image exclusively in WordPerfect, it is advisable to place it immediately in a directory with WordPerfect files. This will save searching time when you need
it.

Subsequently, you are able to retrieve the image as you
normally would in the case of a WordPerfect figure. You
can also further edit it using DrawPerfect, save it again
in .WPG format and then adopt it into WordPerfect.

8.5.2   Graphs from Lotus 1-2-3

Older versions of Lotus 1-2-3 created graphs as .PIC
files. You can adopt these into WordPerfect without any
problem. The .PCX and .CGM files from the more recent 1-2-3 versions can also be used.

8.5.3   Images from DrawPerfect

Images are created in .WPG format in DrawPerfect unless you specify otherwise. This is convenient for Word-
Perfect, conversion is not necessary.

8.5.4   Images from Windows Paintbrush

The Paintbrush program, supplied along with Windows
(in the Accessories group), is capable of saving images
in .BMP and .PCX format. Both can be used in WPWin.
Keep in mind that the DOS versions of WordPerfect,
prior to 5.1, are not capable of supporting the .BMP format. Accordingly, if you wish to exchange files with
WordPerfect 5.1 for DOS, it is better to use the .PCX
format rather than .BMP for images.

8.5.5   Scanned images

There are various hand scanners and flatbed scanners
with the accompanying software on the market. The
software is usually capable of reproducing the scanned
images in different formats. If the .WPG format,
preferred by WordPerfect, is not available, choose
.PCX which can be processed by both WordPerfect and
Windows Paintbrush, as well by various other graphic
programs.

8.5.6   Converting graphic files

There are various programs which are capable of converting graphic files in a certain format to another format. The utility program supplied along with WPWin is
called GRAPHCNV, which is located in the WPWin program directory if you installed the utility programs during
WPWin installation. Otherwise, you will have to do that
now. The program is activated from Windows Program
Manager.

There are also many graphic files in the .GIF format in
the PD and Shareware circuit. There are Shareware
programs which can convert .GIF files to .BMP files.
These can be used in WPWin.

If you frequently work with graphic files, it is advisable to
acquire a professional conversion program such as Hi-
Jaak which is capable of converting from and to more
than 30 different formats.

8.6   Graphic lines

If you wish to place a line between the text, there are a
number of possibilities. WordPerfect distinguishes between the basic line and the line at a certain position.
The basic line has a fixed position on the page. Whether
you enter or remove text before or after the line, the position of the line on the paper remains unchanged. In

the case of a line placed at a certain position, WordPerfect places a code between the text, which moves along
with the text (ensuring that the line also moves) when
the text is altered.

In addition, you can determine the length and thickness
of the line, the horizontal position (left, right or centre),
and the density. 100% black is really black, 75% is dark
grey. Particularly in the case of thick lines, a grey tint is
more pleasant, but the printer must be capable of printing grey tints otherwise the result is not quite so desirable.

To create a horizontal line, proceed as follows:

m   Click on *Graphics*, then *Line*, then *Horizontal*. Normally
the thickness of the line is 0.013" (less than half a mil-
limetre). If you do not wish the line to be so thin, delete
this thickness using Backspace and enter the new thickness.
If you wish to have a different density, click on the arrows under the *Grey Shading* section. If you do not wish
to have a line at a fixed position but wish to have it move
along with the text, click on *Baseline* under *Vertical Position* and choose *Specify*. Click on *Position* and specify
the position of the line in relation to the text. In the same
way, at *Horizontal Position* you can either choose a line
extending across the entire breadth of the page between the margins, or a line at the left, right or centre.

If you select other than the *Full* breadth, you must specify the length of the line at *Length*. When you have concluded the specifications, click on *OK*.

K   Press Alt-G, then L, then H. If you do not wish the line to
be so thin, delete the value in the box and specify a new
thickness. Press Alt-G to specify the line density, va-
rying from 0% (white) to 100% (black). Press Alt-V to
determine the *Vertical Position*. Press Cursor Down to
select another possibility. If you do not wish a line
across the entire breadth, Press Alt-H to change the
Horizontal Position. Using Cursor Down, select one of

the options *Left, Right, Centre, Full* or *Specify*. If you select *Specify*, you must specify where the line should
begin in relation to the left margin. Press Tab once to
specify the position. If you have not selected the *Full*
width option, you can also adjust the length of the line.
Press Alt-O to move to the corresponding window.
When you are satisfied with the specifications, press
Enter.

Vertical lines are determined in the same way, via
Graphics, Line, Vertical. For the *Horizontal Position* you
can choose from the options Left Margin, Right Margin,
Between Columns or Specify.

Exercises

1. Retrieve the REPORT document. Make the head-
    ing extra large. Enter a line between the heading
    and the text and place the cursor between the
    heading and the text. Activate the SAIL_BT.WPG
    image. Place the image 3" from the left margin and
    change the width of the image to 4". Ensure that the
    text from 'Thick' onwards begins 5" from the top of
    the paper. Save the document as REPORT.NW
    and clear the screen.

2. Retrieve the GLASS document. Draw a grey hori-
    zontal line 0.04" thick above and below the text.
    Create space between the heading and the text.
    Place the heading at the end of the line instead of in
    the middle. Save the document as GLASS.NW and
    clear the screen.

Procedures

1. Select *File, Retrieve*. Select **report**. Mark the head-
    ing using Shift-End. Select *Font, Size, Extra Large*.
    Place the cursor between the heading and the
    beginning of the text. Select *Graphics, Retrieve*.
    Select **sail_bt.wpg**. If WordPerfect asks about

hyphenation, choose the *Ignore* option. Click, using the **right** mouse button in the image frame. Then select *Fig. Pos.* The *Box Position and Size* dialogue window appears. Activate the *Horizontal Position* box and change the number to 3. Now activate the *Width* box in the lower left-hand corner. Specify 4". Click on *OK* or press Enter.
Select *File, Save As.* Enter the name **report.nw** and click on *OK* or press Enter. Select *File, Close.*

2. Select *File, Retrieve.* Select **glass**. Place the cursor on the blank line under the heading and press Enter. Select *Graphics, Line, Horizontal.* Change the thickness to 0.04". Click on the bottom button to the right of *Grey Tint* or press the spacebar in order to change the percentage to 50. Click on *OK* or press Enter.
Place the cursor under the text. Press Enter. Select *Graphics, Line, Horizontal.* Again change the thickness to 0.04" and the grey tint density to 50%. Click on *OK* or press Enter.
Mark the heading using Shift-End. Select *Layout, Justification, Right.* Then select *File, Save As.* Enter the name **glass.nw** and click on *OK* or press Enter. Select *File, Close.*

9   Desktop Publishing

9.1   What is desktop publishing?

In practice, this means that a publication is largely formulated using the computer. The size of the publication
may vary from a book or a magazine aimed at thou-
sands of readers, to a letter sent to a single person. Regardless of the number of readers, if the contents are
important in any way, the greatest possible care should
be given to the document.

When we think of desktop publishing, we tend to imagine a situation in which one person produces an entire publication. Certainly with a letter where only one
copy is produced, that will frequently be the case. But,
for instance, with a brochure which will be sent to ten
customers, we can easily imagine that all stages in the
publication will be managed by a single person: writing
the text and making the layout on the personal computer, printing the text on the laser printer, making
photocopies, stapling or binding the pages together,
printing the labels with the addresses and packaging
the brochures for the post. In many cases this way of
working will be efficient and will lead to outstanding results. The person who produces the text and knows
where the publication is going, will probably have a
good idea of the way everything should look.

But this process may take place completely differently.
Not everyone who is capable of producing a good text is
well-acquainted with design and layout or is familiar with
DTP programs. Others may be experts in publication
layout but do not have sufficient feeling for language to
create an interesting text, or may produce many spelling and grammatical errors. In addition, not everyone is
in a situation where a computer, a printer, a photocopy
machine and binding tools are readily available.

Especially in the case of professional publications with
large circulations, the various stages of the publication

process are spread over many people. For instance, a commercial expert indicates the publication topic, a specialized text writer produces the text, a photographer and an artist organize the illustrations, a graphic designer formulates the layout. Then a DTP specialist processes the text file, the scanned photographs and the drawings using advanced devices and programs, and gets the collective product ready for the printer. This is subsequently printed on a photosetting machine, print plates are produced, the publication is printed and the bookbinder makes a nice, neat book(let). If required, mailing specialists are involved in order to send the publication to the proper addresses.

Between the two extremities described above, there are numerous possibilities. We shall presume that, now you have a program providing so many DTP possibilities, you will not only wish to create text, you will also want to arrange the layout. It is important to consider a number of factors in advance.

9.2   Formulating the document

If you have written a text or received it from someone else, you can, of course, just begin on the layout and see what this leads to. If you wish to ensure a satisfactory result and reduce subsequent improvements to a minimum, it is advisable to start by thinking about the layout. Consider the following questions:

■ How many pages of text are there? Will the layout increase this amount?
■ Over how many pages will the text be eventually divided?
■ What is the most useful division?
■ Will the publication have a letter form (a number of pages printed on one side) or a folder or book form (with a deliberately chosen layout in left- and right-hand pages)?
■ If the book form is chosen, will it have a separate cover, or is the first page the front cover?

■ Will each page have the same layout or will this differ
according to page? (Be careful here: the latter option
can produce a rather chaotic impression.)

■ To which parts of the text should the reader's attention be drawn. What are the main themes?

■ Do I expect a reaction? If so, what does the reader require? An address, a telephone number or other information?

■ Is the reader overwhelmed with publications like this
one? Should something particularly striking be included to attract attention?

It is advisable to make a global sketch of the page
layout you have in mind. In this way, you can re-
examine whether this layout is indeed the best for the
goal you wish to achieve.

Do not be surprised if the result is a little disappointing
at first. Some experimentation is needed, certainly at
the beginning. Keep on trying and do not be too easily
contented.

9.3 Improving the layout

Even if you are not a graphic expert, there is no reason
why your letters and reports should not appear orderly
and inviting. A number of points dealing with publications are discussed below.

9.3.1 Legibility

There are factors which obstruct the legibility of printed
texts: letters which are too small, large sections of text
in capitals, a font which is difficult to read. There are of
course more factors requiring attention if you wish to
ensure that the text is inviting to read and will not be too
easily shoved aside:

■ Make a clear division into paragraphs. Open space
between the paragraphs improves the overall layout

and, accordingly, the legibility. A line spacing of around 1.6 or 1.8 between the last line of the previous paragraph and the beginning of the following one is the best. In a text with many paragraphs this may mean that line spacing often has to be altered. This problem can be solved by making macros, for example for line spacings of 1.1 and 1.75 and then setting these macros in the button bar. However, you can also simply give two hard returns (twice Enter) at the end of the paragraph so that a blank line is produced.

■ Do not make the pages too full. The 1" margins, the WP default setting, are not exaggerated. You can reduce them, but in many cases there are good arguments for making them even larger.

■ Nevertheless, if you do use a small font, consider the possibility of placing text in columns so that the lines are not too long.

9.3.2 Page layout

The following suggestions may help to effect a pleasant page layout:

■ Ensure a clear line throughout the document, also in the visual aspect. Both horizontal and vertical lines should be recognizable in the page layout, even if they are not actually visible. They provide the basis for an orderly layout.

■ Use sufficient space. A mistake easily made by users who are graphically inexperienced is to try to get too much onto the page. It is better to enlarge the margins rather than reduce them, especially when dealing with presentation material where it defeats the purpose to try to save a sheet of paper. The default margin settings are 1" at each side and this is sufficient for a business letter. In the case of a more official letter which will be sent to a large number of readers, or of a book(let) with a more representative nature, it is advisable to increase the margins. According to the classic rules for typefacing (which are not always adhered to), the sum of both margins should equal the width of the text. This means that on a normal type sheet, left and right margins of two inches are not out of place. It does not always have to be symmetrical, you can, for instance, have two and a half and one and a half. In addition, the top and bottom margins may also exceed 1".

9.3.3   Variation

A change is as good as a rest, as the proverb goes. This also applies to a publication. You can vary the layout, but do not do this too often since it will give the document as a whole a rather chaotic appearance. Remember that dynamic advertising requires more variation than an official or scientific report. What can be done to bring a little variation?

- The presence of a right margin need not automatically mean that the text is fully right-aligned. It is possible to vary within one publication if there are differing texts and not one continuous text. You can fully justify one text (left- and right-aligned) and left-align another (thus without a straight right-hand edge). Too much variation, however, leads to confusion.
  For instance, you can left-align all texts with the exception of one text (preferably the longest) which can be fully aligned.
- It is also unnecessary to set all the headings in exactly the same way. You could centre the largest headings and left-align the smaller ones.
- An asymmetrical layout gives a more dynamic impression. A symmetrical layout is more conservative and thus makes a solid impression. For a dynamic presentation you could place lengthy sections of text in three columns, or in one narrow and two broad columns (one third and two thirds of the page width).
- Pay attention to the information concerning fonts in chapter 6.

9.3.4 Attracting attention

Perhaps you wish to draw the reader's attention to certain sections of the text in particular. Or you wish to give the whole publication a striking appearance. Keep the following points in mind:

■ Use frames and borders to accentuate things. Normally, the most noticeable part of the text is that which begins at the top left of the page, especially when it also has a large heading. If you wish to have something else emphasized, place it lower down on the page with a border around it. If necessary, use a different font for the text in the frame. This may be another font or another size, or for instance, italics instead of the normal version. If the remainder of the text on the page is only left-aligned, you could fully align the text in question in order to make it more conspicuous.

■ Use an illustration to attract the reader's attention. A picture is sometimes worth more than a thousand words. You should use a good quality illustration which suits the subject matter. Omit an illustration rather choose a poor one. In addition, if the printer does not reproduce illustrations well, it may be better not to use them since this may make an amateuristic impression on the reader.

■ Do not use too many garish elements on the same page. This becomes chaotic and tedious and will tend to repel readers.

■ Some blank space before and after an important section of text helps to accentuate the text.

9.3.5 Use styles to make it easy for yourself

If you use a certain layout regularly, make it into a **style**. In this way you can design new documents much more quickly. WordPerfect provides a quartet of standard styles. Using these provides a convenient method of achieving a satisfactory result without too much difficulty. You can easily create new styles yourself.

There are *open* and *paired* styles. In the case of an open style, you can specify the style and then begin typing text. The set style applies to all subsequent entries. In the case of a *paired* style, you must first select or mark the text and then activate the style. The paired style determines the appearance of the text and also (to a certain extent) the appearance of subsequent text.

Try one of the styles supplied along with WordPerfect:

M   Click on *Layout*, then *Styles*. A window containing four styles appears. Select **Tech Init** by double clicking on it.

K   Press Alt-F8. Mark the **Tech Int** style using the Cursor Down key. Press Enter.

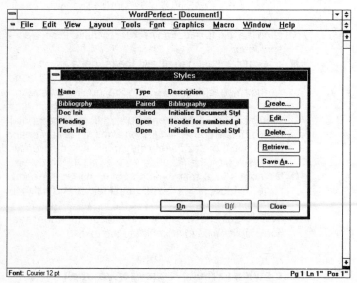

Type several words then press Enter. You will observe that a large number 1 has appeared. Type several more words, press Enter and you will notice that the letters now appear considerably smaller on the screen. If you press Enter once more, a number is shown again, this time a 2. Type more words and press Enter now and again. As you will observe at the bottom of the screen, automatic paragraph numeration has been installed with this style. In addition, the setting in this style specifies that the one paragraph receives a large, bold letter and the following a standard letter.

You can create new styles yourself. As an exercise, we shall take a text for a heading which should be large, bold and centred. Ensure (using the *View* menu) that the display of *Comments* is switched on.

m   Click on *Layout*, then *Styles*. A list of existing styles will be displayed. Click on *Create*. Enter the name: **heading**. Click on the box under *Description*. Enter: **bold, large, centred**. Click on *OK*.

K   Press Alt-F8. A list of existing styles will appear. Press Alt-C. Enter the name: **heading**. Press Tab, enter the *Description*: **bold, large, centred**. Press Enter.

You will now see a partitioned window. Comments are placed in the upper section. Using Cursor Left and Cursor Right, you can move the cursor to in front of or behind the comments. Codes are shown in the lower section. At the moment there is only the code [Comment]. We shall create a paired style. This means that the appropriate formatting codes are switched on at the beginning of the style and are switched off again at the end. Ensure that the cursor is first placed above the comments. Press Ctrl-B in order to switch on the bold feature, then on Shift-F7 (DOS keyboards Shift-F6) to activate the centre function and then on Ctrl-S, L in order to activate the large feature. Move the cursor to behind the comments by pressing Cursor right. Using the same key combinations, you can place codes in order to switch off the selected functions once more. Click on *Close* twice or press Alt-C and using the Tab key, move to *Close* and press Enter.

You can allocate this style to a section of text by first selecting the text and then switching on the relevant style using the *Layout, Styles* menu.

10   WordPerfect File Manager

10.1   Activating the WordPerfect File Manager from Windows

You can activate the WordPerfect File Manager from both Windows and WPWin. From Windows, activate it as follows:

m   Click on *Window*, then on *WordPerfect*, double click on *File Manager*.

K   Press Alt-W, type the underlined number in front of WordPerfect, highlight the File Manager using Cursor Right and press Enter.

10.2   Activating the File Manager from WordPerfect

Although the File Manager is a separate program, you can activate it directly from WordPerfect.

m   Click on *File*, click on *File Manager*.

K   Press Alt-F, press F.

D   Press F5.

10.3   The WordPerfect File Manager window

When you have activated the File Manager, it should appear as shown below:

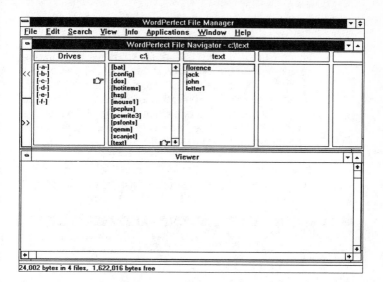

24,002 bytes in 4 files, 1,622,016 bytes free

There are two windows within the File Manager window: Navigator and Viewer. The Navigator helps you to find the correct path from one directory to the other. The Viewer displays a part of the file contents.

10.4 The Navigator

Imagine, for instance, that you are looking for a file in a subsubdirectory.

M Double click on [-c-] in the Drives list (or on another required disk). A list of directories and files on C: is shown adjacent to the Drives list. By clicking on the small arrows at the top and bottom of the scroll bar next to this list, you can browse through the entire contents. Double click on the name of the required directory. Another list will appear showing the names of the subdirectories and files in the selected directory. Double click on the name of a subdirectory. Another list will appear. Double click on the name of the required subdirectory here too. At the extreme right, a new list is displayed while the other lists move over to the left.

Move to the required disk using the cursor keys. Press Enter. A list of directories and files on C: will appear. Using Cursor Up and Cursor Down, move to the name of the appropriate directory. Press Enter. A new list will show the names of the subdirectories and files in the selected directory. Highlight the required directory and press Enter. Repeat these steps. Finally, at the extreme right-hand side, a new list will be displayed, while the other lists move over to the left.

If you click once on the name of a file or mark a file using the cursor keys, the first section of the contents of that file will be shown in the Viewer window.

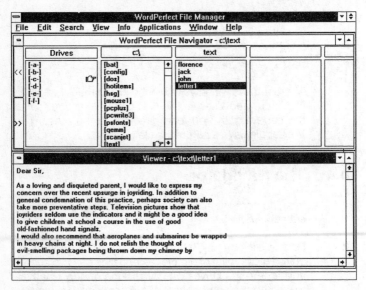

10.5   The Viewer

Do you wish to examine the contents of a file more closely?

Click on the (as yet blank) title bar of the Viewer. Click on the control menu button of this window (at the left of

the title bar). Click on the *Maximize* option. Using the
scroll bar at the right, you can now examine the rest of
the file.

ᛘ Press Alt-W. Type the number which is in front of the
Viewer option in the *View* menu. Use Cursor Down to
move through the file text in the Viewer.

In order to return to the Navigator window, proceed as
follows:

ᛘ Click on the control menu button of the innermost window, next to the menu bar. Click on *Restore*. Click on
the Navigator title bar.

ᛘ Press Alt-W. Type the number which is shown in front of
the WordPerfect File Navigator.

10.6   File management

Copying, moving and deleting files is quite easily done.

ᛘ Click once on the file name. Click on one of the buttons
on the button bar: *Copy, Delete* or *Move*. Answer the
questions in the dialogue box, activate the options if required and click on *OK*.

ᛘ Mark the file using Tab and the cursor keys. Press Alt-F.
Select one of the options from the *File* menu, answer
the questions in the dialogue box (remember that you
can move to other text boxes using Tab and you can set
or remove crosses next to the options using the spacebar), press Enter or press Esc if you wish to try again.

The *File* menu also enables you to print texts, create a
new directory or adjust the printer settings. You can
also activate programs by highlighting the program
name and selecting the *Run* option from the *File* menu.

In addition, you can also open text files or other data
files from the Navigator. Highlight the relevant file, click

on *Open* in the button list. If this is a WordPerfect file, WPWin will be activated and the chosen file will be immediately loaded. If this is not a WordPerfect file, a dialogue box will ask to which program the file belongs, so that the appropriate program can be activated.

10.7   The file list

The File Manager list of files strongly resembles the file list in WordPerfect 5.1 under DOS. How is this displayed on the screen?

m   Click on the name of a disk or directory in one of the Navigator windows lists in order to show the list of files belonging to this disk or directory.

K   Press Alt-V, then F.

The File List shows under Filename the names of files and (sub)directories on a disk or in a directory. Under Size, [DIR] is displayed to indicate a directory, and the number of bytes used is shown if it is a file. Under Date, the system date is shown for the date when the file was created or most recently altered, and under Time the system time is shown for the moment that this took place.

You can change the layout of the file list using the mouse. For instance, if you do not wish to see the time, click on the Time button and drag it away from the button bar. If you wish to have the date at the left of the button bar, drag the Date button to left side of the bar. If you wish to see the file attributes (a, h, r and/or s), click on an empty space in the bar. A menu will appear from which you can select the Attributes option. You may add a description to the file names, or divide them into topics. Using the same menu (activate it by clicking on a free part of it), you can add buttons (and thus columns) for doing this.

When you are finished using the File List:

M Click on the Navigator title bar. The File List window is
then closed.

K Press Alt-W and type the number in front of Navigator.

10.8 Activating WordPerfect from the File Manager

It is not necessary to exit the File Manager, if you have
activated it directly from Windows, in order to begin
working with WordPerfect. WordPerfect can be activated directly from the File Manager.

M Click on *Applications*, click on *WordPerfect*. WordPerfect appears in a window with the file which was last
shown in the Viewer window. Click on the WordPerfect
control menu button and then on *Maximize* if you wish
to work extensively on the text. When you exit WordPerfect, you will return to the File Manager.

K Press Alt-A, mark WordPerfect using Cursor Down,
press Enter. WordPerfect appears in a window. If you
wish to continue with WordPerfect, press Alt-spacebar
and type X (for *Maximize*). When you exit WordPerfect,
you will return to the File Manager.

Avoid complicated, memory-consuming situations like
opening the File Manager, starting WordPerfect from
the File Manager etc. Then WordPerfect will run in a
window of a program which runs within a window of
WordPerfect! If you have activated the File Manager via
WordPerfect, return to WordPerfect by closing the File
Manager, and vice versa.

10.9   Closing the File Manager

If you do not wish to continue with the File Manager, proceed as follows:

M   Click on *File*, then *Close*.

K   Press Alt-F4.

D   Press F7.

10.10 Additional options

There is not enough space within the scope of this book to discuss all the possibilities of the File Manager. You can discover them yourself using the menus and the button bar. By now you will be familiar with selecting options, specifying boxes etc. If you wish to cancel an option, this can often be done by pressing Esc. Information about the possibilities can always be gained by pressing F1 (Help).

11   More special functions

11.1   Advancing text to a specific position

The Advance feature in WordPerfect for Windows enables you to place text on a page with great accuracy. A distinction is made between horizontal and vertical advance and also between advancement over a certain distance and advancement to a certain position.

Advancement over a certain distance is used when you wish to determine a fixed space between two sections of text. If you have typed a line of text and you wish to begin the following line 3" lower, proceed as follows:

M   Click on *Layout*, click on *Advance*. Click on *Down*. Click on the text window and enter **3"** or **3 in**. Click on *OK*.

K   Press Alt-L, then A. Press Cursor Down in order to move to *Down*. Press Tab. At *Advance* specify **3"** or **3 in**. Press Enter.

D   Press Shift-F8, press A. Press Cursor Down to move to *Down*. Press Tab. At *Advance* specify **3"** or **3 in**. Press Enter.

The cursor will now be 3 inches lower (see status bar).

The Advance function can be extremely useful for filling in forms. You must first measure the distance from the top and from the left-hand side of the paper, of every box which is to be filled in. The specified position will approximately conform to the top left-hand corner of the letter **v** or the letter **x** when printed. If you wish to be sure that it is perfectly accurate, first examine if there is no inherent deviation to the right, left, above or below in your printer.

Example: we shall use a macro to put an address on a letter which is to be sent in a window envelope. The macro puts comments at the position where the name, address and postal code should be.

Measurement has determined that the position of the address is:

■ between 2" and 3" from the top of the paper,
■ between 4" and 8" from the left edge.

Of course the address should not appear in the corner of the envelope window. A little space will be left open.

𝓜　　Click on *Macro*, click on *Record*. Specify the macro name: ADDRESS and click on *Record*. (You may enter a Description and/or an Abstract if required.) The statement *Recording Macro* is displayed at the left-hand side of the status bar.

Click on *Layout, Advance, Down*. Click on the *Advance* box, enter 2.5" and click on *OK*.

Click on *Layout, Advance, To Position*. Click on *Advance*, enter 4.5" and click on *OK*.

Click on *Tools, Comment, Create*. Type **name:** and click on *OK*. Press Enter to move to the next line.

Click on *Layout, Advance, To Position*. Click on *Advance*, enter 4.5" and click on *OK*.

Click on *Tools, Comment, Create*. Type **address:** and click on *OK*. Press Enter to move to the next line.

Click on *Layout, Advance, To Position*. Click on *Advance*, enter 4.5" and click on *OK*.

Click on *Tools, Comment, Create*. Type **post code:** and click on *OK*. Press Enter to quit the line.

Click on *Macro*, then *Stop*.

𝓚　　Press Ctrl-F10. Enter the macro name: ADDRESS and press Enter unless you wish to specify a description or an abstract. The message *Recording Macro* appears at the left of the status bar.

Press Alt-L, then A. Press Alt-D, then Tab, enter 2.5" and press Enter.

Press Alt-L, then A. Press Alt-P, then Tab, enter 4.5" and press Enter.

Press Alt-T, then N, then C. Type **name:** and press Enter. Press Enter again to move to the next line.

Press Alt-L, then A. Press Alt-P, then Tab, enter 4.5"
and press Enter.
Press Alt-T, then N, then C. Type **address:** and press
Enter. Press Enter again to move to the next line.
Press Alt-L, then A. Press Alt-P, then Tab, enter 4.5"
and press Enter.
Press Alt-T, then N, then C. Type **post code:** and
press Enter. Now press Enter to quit the line with the
address.
Press Ctrl-Shift-F10.

The macro is now complete. When you wish to place an
address on a letter, activate the ADDRESS macro. You
can also assign this macro to the Macro menu if you are
going to use it a lot. To enter the name and address at
the proper position each time, you only need to position
the cursor under the comment line containing 'name:'
and specify the name. Fill in the address and the postal
code in the same way.
A disadvantage of this macro is that no other address
information can be given exceeding the one line for
each category (name, address, postal code). In the
exercises at the end of this chapter, a macro will be created in which you can specify more information.

11.2   Creating tables

If you import data (using *Tools, Spreadsheet*) from a
spreadsheet which has been made using PlanPerfect,
Lotus 1-2-3, Excel 3.0 or more recent, or Quattro, these
will automatically be formulated in a table. Tables can
also be created using the Tables function.

m   Press *Layout, Tables, Create.* As you will observe, the
default setting is 3 columns and only one row. If necessary, alter the number of columns, click on the box next
to *Rows*, remove the 1 and specify the required number
of rows. Click on *OK*.

k   Press Ctrl-F9, then Enter. Or press Alt-L, then T, then
C. Replace the 3 with the required amount of columns,

press Tab, replace the 1 with the required amount of rows and press Enter.

⟳   Press Alt-F7 and select *Create*. Or press Alt-L, then T then C. Replace the 3 with the required amount of columns, press Tab, replace the 1 with the required amount of rows and press Enter.

You may enter text, numbers or images in any cell of the table. The size of the cell is automatically adjusted if the text does not fit onto one line or if you place an image in the table. Within a cell, you can align the text or centre it, as required. Using Tab or the cursor keys, you move the cursor to another cell.
If you wish to have extra rows or columns in an existing table, select *Layout, Tables, Insert*. Specify how many rows or columns should be inserted and press Enter or click on *OK*.
New rows or columns are inserted in front of the cell in which the cursor is currently located.

There are numerous methods of editing a table. Using *Tables, Options*, you can alter the margins within cells and apply grey tints. Other possibilities using *Tables* include splitting a single cell (thus without an extra column being inserted in the length), joining cells (first mark the relevant cells before selecting the *Join* option), deleting rows or columns (the row or column in which the cursor is currently located and subsequent rows or columns if necessary), adjustment of the cell format, adjustment of the row or column format, for instance, displaying the text in all cells of a particular row in italics or bold, or centred or large. If you wish to do this in a number of rows or columns simultaneously, mark the relevant columns or rows before selecting the *Cell Format* or *Column Format* option.
The *Lines* option in the *Tables* menu enables you to replace single lines with double or vice versa, or to completely remove the lines between certain rows or columns.

11.3   Adjusting the table frame

If you wish to determine the exact size and position of the table, use the *Table Box* function. When you use this function, WordPerfect will ask which *editor* you wish to use. This will normally be the Text Editor.

M   Click on *Graphics, Table Box, Create*. Click on *OK* to accept the default editor. Click on *Box Position*. The *Box Position and Size* dialogue box is displayed. *Vertical Position* and *Horizontal Position* indicate the position of the start of the table in relation to the top of the page. You can alter this if required. You can specify the *Width* in the *Size* box at the bottom. The *Height* is determined automatically. You can also do this in reverse order: click on *Width* (*Auto Height*) and choose vice versa, Auto Both or Set Both. Click on the option button next to 'Wrap Text Around Box' if you do not wish the rest of the text to be placed around the box. When everything is to your satisfaction, click on *OK*.

K   Press Alt-G, press T, then C. Press Enter to accept the default editor. Press Alt-P in order to specify the position and size of the box. You can move between options using Tab. At the *Wrap Text Around Box* option, you can place or remove a cross by pressing the spacebar. This determines whether the text is placed around the table. Options which are not (only) specified by entering numbers can be altered by using Cursor Up and Cursor Down. When eveything is to your satisfaction, press Enter. Press Alt-C to return to the text.

11.4   Creating tables using the Ruler

If you are working with a mouse, you can make tables very quickly using the Ruler. If the Ruler is not currently displayed, click on *View, Ruler*. Click on the box with gridlines in the Ruler, hold the mouse button down and move the mouse down to the right so that the required number of rows and columns is visible. The corresponding table will be created immediately.

11.5   Framing a text using a table

You can use the Table function to place a frame around
a created text. This is more convenient than using the
Text Box function. Create a table consisting of one row
and one column, at the position where the text frame
should come. Mark the section of text which you wish to
place in the frame. Press Shift-Del to move the text.
Place the cursor in the created table which now consists
of one cell. Press Shift-Ins to retrieve the text. The text
will be placed in the frame. If you wish to centre the text
or display it in a larger font or bold, select the text within
the table and select the appropriate function.

If the frame is too broad, you can edit it using the Table
Box function (see above). If you wish to have single
lines instead of double, you can regulate this using
Layout, Tables, Lines.

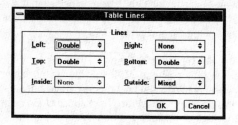

11.6   The Merge feature

The Merge feature is normally used for form letters, but,
as we shall see in chapter 13, there are more possibilities. In the following outline, we shall work with an
address file and a form letter. The text of the letter, in
which codes indicate the the position of the name, address etc, is referred to in WordPerfect as the primary
file. The list containing names, addresses etc is called
the secondary file.

More examples of merging files and explanation of the
terminology can be found in chapter 13.

11.6.1 Creating a form letter

The form letter (the primary merge file) is made just as any common letter. Only the name, the address and other particular data are not entered. These are replaced by codes.

In this process, we refer to **fields**. For example, the name is a field, the address is a field, the introduction *Dear Sir/Madam* is also a field.

How do you indicate that a certain field is to be adopted in a letter?

m Click on *Tools, Merge, Field*. A dialogue box will request the name of the field. Fill this in, for example, *name*, and press Enter.

K Press Ctrl-F12, then F. Specify the field name, for example *name* and press Enter.

D Press Shift-F9, then F. Specify the field name, for example, *name* and press Enter.

In your document you will now see {FIELD}name~. When the merge is implemented, the field which you have called *name* in the secondary file will be placed here.

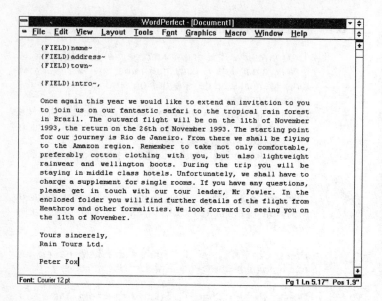

```
(FIELD)name~
(FIELD)address~
(FIELD)town~

(FIELD)intro~,

Once again this year we would like to extend an invitation to you
to join us on our fantastic safari to the tropical rain forest
in Brazil. The outward flight will be on the 11th of November
1993, the return on the 26th of November 1993. The starting point
for our journey is Rio de Janeiro. From there we shall be flying
to the Amazon region. Remember to take not only comfortable,
preferably cotton clothing with you, but also lightweight
rainwear and wellington boots. During the trip you will be
staying in middle class hotels. Unfortunately, we shall have to
charge a supplement for single rooms. If you have any questions,
please get in touch with our tour leader, Mr Fowler. In the
enclosed folder you will find further details of the flight from
Heathrow and other formalities. We look forward to seeing you on
the 11th of November.


Yours sincerely,
Rain Tours Ltd.

Peter Fox
```

11.6.2   Creating an address list

The list of addresses and other data is referred to as the secondary merge file. How is this list made? We assume that it consists of the name, address, town and introduction fields. In the first example, these names are not yet in use. The fields will simply be called Field1, Field2 etc.

M   Create a new document. Type a name as it should be registered in the address, for example *Sir Billy Binkerhill*. Click on *Tools, Merge, End Field*.
Type an address, for example *Binkerhill Mansion*. Click on *Tools, Merge, End Field*.
Type the town, for example, *Dochester*. Click on *Tools, Merge, End Field*.
Type the introduction to the letter, for example, *Dear Bill*. Click on *Tools, Merge, End Record*.

K   Create a new document. Type the name as it should be registered in the address, for example, *Sir Billy Binker-*

hill. Press Ctrl-F12 and then Enter, or directly on Alt-Enter.

Type the address, for example, *Binkerhill Mansion.* Press Alt-Enter.

Type the town, for example *Dochester.* Press Alt-Enter.

Type the introduction, for example, *Dear Bill.* Press Ctrl-F12 and type an R, or press directly Alt-Shift-Enter.

D Create a new document. Type the name as it should be registered in the address, for example *Sir Billy Binker-hill.* Press F9.

Type the address, for example *Binkerhill Mansion.* Press F9.

Type the town, for example, *Dochester.* Press F9.

Type the introduction, for example *Dear Bill.* Press Shift-F9, type an R.

You have now created one record. If you wish to make more records (comparable to the cards in a card index), repeat this procedure. At the bottom of the screen on the status bar, you will see the messages Field:1, Field:2 etc.

Immediately assigning names makes working with fields clearer. Proceed as follows (after having created a new document):

M Click on *Tools, Merge, Merge Codes.*

K Press Alt-T, M, then C.

Scroll down until the {FIELD NAMES} code is high-lighted. Choose *Insert* by clicking on it or by pressing Tab and Enter. A box will state that the current field is number 1. Specify a field name: **name** and click on *Add* or press Alt-A. Specify the following field name: **ad-dress** and click on *Add* or press Alt-A. In the same way, specify the **town** and **intro(duction)** fields. Click on *OK* or press Enter and click on *Close*, or press Tab and when Close is highlighted, press Enter.

A list of field names is shown at the top of your document. At the bottom, you will observe *{FIELD NAMES}name~~.*

Now specify a name and press Alt-Enter. At the bottom of the screen, you will now see *Field:address.* Specify an address and press Alt-Enter. At the bottom, *Field:town* is shown. Specify the town and press Alt-Enter. Specify the introduction and press Alt-Shift-Enter.

Specify a name and press F9. At the bottom, *Field:ad-dress* is shown. Specify the address and press F9. At the bottom, *Field:town* is shown. Specify the town and press F9. Specify the introduction, press Shift-F9 and type an R.

As you may have noticed, placing the {END FIELD} and {END RECORD} codes using the mouse is rather laborious. For this reason, it is advisable to make a button bar for merging in which *End Field* and *End Record* occur.

```
                       WordPerfect - [Document2]                    ▼ ♦
 ▪ File  Edit  View  Layout  Tools  Font  Graphics  Macro  Window  Help   ♦
     {FIELD NAMES}name~address~town~intro~~{END RECORD}               ♦

     Sir Billy Binkerhill{END FIELD}
     Binkerhill Mansion{END FIELD}
     Dochester{END FIELD}
     Dear Bill{END RECORD}

     Mr Richard Granger{END FIELD}
     19 High Dyke{END FIELD}
     Taunton{END FIELD}
     Dear Richard{END RECORD}




                                                                      ♦
 Field: name                                          Pg 4 Ln 1" Pos 1"
```

11.6.3 Merging

When the primary file (form letter) and the secondary file (address list) have been completed, you can proceed with the merge.
Begin a new document.

M Click on *Tools, Merge, Merge*. Specify the name of the Primary file (the letter). If you do not remember the name anymore, click on the button at the right of the text box and you will be able to search for the name of the file. When the name has been specified, click on *Select* and then move to the box for the Secondary file. Enter the name of the address list here. Click on *OK*.

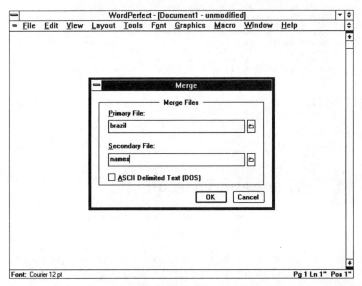

K Press Ctrl-F12, then M. Specify the name of the Primary file (the letter). Press Tab and enter the name of the Secondary file (the addresses). Press Enter.

D Press Shift-F9 and then M. Specify the name of the Primary file (the letter). Press Tab and enter the name of the Secondary file (the address list). Press Enter.

There are now just as many letters as there were addresses in the secondary file. Each letter begins on a new page, so that they can be printed on separate sheets of paper. Because all the letters are in one file, one print instruction is sufficient to print them all.

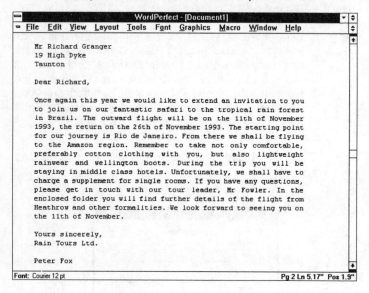

11.7 Numbering paragraphs

The paragraphs in your text can be automatically numbered.

M   Click on *Tools, Outline, Define*. Select a Style for the numeration: Roman or Arabic numbers, capitals or small letters. This is done by clicking on the button next to the Style selection box and then clicking on the required style. You will observe a cross in the Outline On box. Leave this unaltered if you wish the paragraph numeration to take immediate effect. Click on *OK*.

K   Press Alt-T, then O, then D. Press Tab once to move to the Style box. Alter the contents of the box according to

the desired style of numbering. You will observe a cross
in the Outline On box. Leave this unaltered if you wish
the paragraph numeration to take immediate effect.
Press Enter.

Each time you press Enter when typing your document,
a new line with an ascending number will be begun. If
you insert a paragraph, the numeration will be adjusted
automatically.

It is often more desirable to place the numbers at positions where you explicitly wish to have them. This is
referred to as manual numeration. In this, you have the
advantage of being able to work at different levels. For
instance, you can number the chapters in your text as I.,
II., III. etc, the paragraphs within the chapters as A., B.,
C. etc and the sections as 1., 2., 3. etc. Or perhaps you
prefer the so-called legal style. The chapters are then
numbered as 1, 2, 3 etc., the subdivision is then 1.1,
1.2, 1.3 etc and the subdivision of for instance 2.2 is
2.2.1, 2.2.2, 2.2.3 etc. This style is used in this book. In
order to specify this style, proceed as follows:

M   Click on *Tools, Outline, Define*. Click on *Outline* then on
Legal. Click on the box next to *Attach Previous Level*.
Click on *Enter Inserts Paragraph number* to remove the
cross. This ensures that the numbers are only placed at
the positions you specify. Click on *OK*.

K   Press Alt-T, O, then D. Using Cursor Down and Cursor
Up, select the default format, Legal. Press Tab twice to
move to *Attach Previous Level*. Press the spacebar to
place a cross there. Press Alt-E to remove the cross next
to *Enter Inserts Paragraph Number*, so that the numeration does not automatically continue when you press
Enter while working on your document. Now press Enter.

How do you insert a paragraph number?

M   Click on *Tools, Outline, Paragraph Numbering*. Click on
Manual. The number shown registers the level of numbering. Alter this if required. Click on *Insert*.

K   Press Alt-F5. then M. Press Tab if you wish to alter the
level of numbering. Press Enter.

D   Press Shift-F5, then P. Press Alt-M. Press Tab if you
wish to alter the level of numbering. Press Enter.

If you frequently use the paragraph numbering, is is
very useful to make a button in the button bar for *Paragraph Numbering*. You can work even more quickly if
you create macros for level 1, level 2 etc. and place
these in the button bar.

11.8   Table of contents: definition

If you use WordPerfect to make a report, an essay or a
course manual, it can be useful to add a table of contents. Consider first whether you wish to have this table
of contents at the beginning or the end. Place the cursor
there and now specify the appearance of the table of
contents.

M   Click on *Tools, Define, Table of Contents*. Define the
number of levels (maximum of 5).

K   Press Alt-T, then F, then C. Define the number of levels
(maximum of 5).

For example: level 1 is for the chapters, level 2 is for the
titles of the paragraphs, level 3 is for the titles of the
subparagraphs etc. Make a selection from the options
provided for each level: page numeration yes/no, dot
leaders or brackets yes/no etc. An example is given in
the right-hand section of the Numbering Style window.
The final level can also be specified as being 'in
wrapped format':

```
Task definition (25) Problem analysis (25)
Program flow diagram (26) Coding (28)
Testing the program (39) Program
documentation (50)
```

To do this, you must ensure that a cross has been placed next to *Last Level In Wrapped Format*. If you also wish to have the subparagraphs at this level under one another, ensure that no cross has been set.

𝓜   Specify manually the number of levels or click on the arrows next to the corresponding text box. Click on the available settings registered at Level 1, Level 2 etc. in order to examine the possibilities and to make a selection. Click on the option button in the lower left-hand corner if you wish to have a continuous format at the final level. Click on *OK*.

𝓚   Specify the required number of levels. Press Tab to move to Level 1. Using Cursor Up and Cursor Down, choose the appropriate format. Press Tab to move to the next level. The option button in the lower left-hand corner can be filled in or made empty by pressing the spacebar. Press Enter when you have made all the required selections.

11.9   Marking for the table of contents

Now you must specify in your document which sections of text are to be placed in the table of contents. You may choose any sections of text for this, although the headings and subheadings are the obvious choices. First select the line of text which is to be placed in the table of contents.

𝓜   Click on *Tools, Mark Text, Table of Contents*. You will be asked to which level in the table of contents this text should be assigned. Specify a number (but not greater than the number of levels you have defined!) and click on *OK*.

𝓚   Press Alt-T, then K, then C. Specify the level in which the marked text should appear in the table of contents (do not enter a number larger than the specified number of levels). Press Enter.

Now look for the next text which should appear in the table of contents and repeat the above procedure. If you have to mark a lot of text, it is convenient to have the *Mark Text/Table of Contents* function in the button bar. Making macros for Level 1, Level 2 etc. and setting these in the button bar is even more useful.

11.10 Generating a table of contents

WordPerfect creates the table of contents completely automatically. In the case of long documents, it may be time-consuming. If you place the table of contents at the beginning, reserve a separate page for it by pressing Ctrl-Enter after defining the contents. If it becomes a rather lengthy table of contents and there is a chance that you may have to arrange the contents over two pages, reserve an extra page by pressing Ctrl-Enter twice after defining the contents. Keep in mind that you must not alter the text after creating the table of contents, otherwise the page numbering will no longer correspond.

m   Click on *Tools, Generate, Yes*. The table of contents will appear on the screen after a moment.

K   Press Alt-T, then G and press Enter. The table of contents will appear on the screen after a moment.

If you wish, you can give the table of contents a more elegant design, but remember that the first registered page containing text must retain the same number.
If you are forced to change something in the text of your document, and this results in alteration of the page layout, have the table of contents generated again.

11.11 Making an index: definition

An index of important words or concepts in the text can be useful in large documents. The index layout can also be made in various ways. The index is normally placed at the end of the document.

m   Click on *Tools, Define, Index.* You may choose between different styles of numbering. Samples are displayed on the screen when you select them. When you have found the right style, click on *OK.*

K   Press Alt-T, then F, then I. Using Cursor Up or Cursor Down, you can highlight the numbering styles. Samples are displayed on the screen. When you have made your choice, press Enter.

11.12   Marking for the index

How do you indicate that a certain word or term should be included in the index?

m   Click on the word. Click on *Tools, Mark Text, Index.* A box appears in which you can specify a heading and subheading for the index item. You can select only the heading or specify both. Click on *OK.*

K   Place the cursor on the word and press Alt-T, then K, then I. Specify the heading under which the text should be placed in the index, and a subheading if required (move to it using Tab). Press Enter.

The word on which the cursor is currently positioned is adopted as the heading unless you replace it with another word or words. Then it is defined as a subheading, but here also, you may specify something else.

If, for instance, the word *mouse* occurs in the text, you can include the word mouse on its own in the index. If there are more references to *mouse*, you have more possibilities. You could make entries under the headings *computer mouse* and *field mouse* in the index. But you could also include them under one heading, *mouse*, with subheadings *computer* and *field*.

11.13 Generating the index

Do not generate the index before the entire text is completed, otherwise the page numbering will no longer correspond. If the text also includes marking for the table of contents, this will also be generated. This takes place using the menu options *Tools, Generate, Yes*.

If WPWin tends to be a little slow on your computer and you have to generate the table of contents and the index for a lengthy document, this can be very time-consuming. If you also have WordPerfect 5.1 for DOS, it may be quicker to generate the table of contents and the index in the DOS version. Keep in mind that the DOS version may have problems if an index code occurs in the middle of section of text which is marked for the table of contents. If this can occur, it is advisable to allow WPWin to carry out the generation after all.

Exercises

1.   Create a macro to place a random amount of addresses at the proper position on a letter which is to be put into a window envelope. The address should be 2.5" from the top of the paper and 4.75" from the left-hand edge. Comments should be used to define the position where the address is to be typed. Assign the name ADDRESS2 to the macro.

2.   Retrieve the REPORT.NW file. Move the image 0.5" to the left. Have the actual text (from the second 'Thick') begin *under* the image, 5" from the top edge of the paper. Save the file again as REPORT.NW.

3.   Retrieve the TWINREP file. Set the line spacing to 1.1. Change the margins to 3, 3, 3, and 4 (at the bottom). Confine the text to one page. Place a frame under the report text and place the glass text in it. Save the file as TWINREP3.

Procedures

1. Select *Macro, Record*. Specify the name **ad-dress2**. Select *Record*. Select *Layout, Advance, Down*. Activate the *Advance* box and specify 2.5". Press Enter. Select *Layout, Margins*. Change the left-hand margin to 4.75" and the right-hand margin to 1.5". Confirm using *OK* or Enter.
    Select *Tools, Comment, Create*. Fill in the Comment window: Beginning name and address. Click on *OK* or press Enter. Press Enter again.
    Select *Tools, Comment, Create*. Fill in: End address. Click on *OK* or press Enter. Select *Layout, Margins*. Restore the left and right margins to 1". Click on *OK* or press Enter. Select *Macro, Stop*.
    When the macro is run, place the cursor *between* the two lines of comments and type the address, pressing Enter as normally between each address line. The margins which have been temporarily altered ensure that the address is placed in the correct position.

2. Select *File, Retrieve*. Select **report.nw**. Click on the picture using the right mouse button and activate *Box Position* to select Position and Size. Activate the *Horizontal Position* box and change the position to 6. Activate the *Wrap Text Around Box* option button and remove the cross by clicking on it or pressing the spacebar. Click on *OK* or press Enter. The text now runs through the image. Place the cursor in front of 'Thick' and select *Layout, Advance, Down*. Activate the *Advance* box, specify 5" and click on *OK* or press Enter. Select *File, Save*, and specify the name, REPORT.NW. Select *File, Close*.

3. Select *File, Retrieve*. Select **twinrep**. Press Alt-F3 to display the codes. Remove the codes for the margins and the line spacing which are located near the beginning. Press Alt-F3 once more.
    Ensure that the cursor is placed at the beginning of the heading. Select *Layout, Margins* and change

the margins to 3, 3, 3 and 4 and click on *OK* or press Enter. Select *Layout, Line, Spacing*. Change this to 1.1 and click on *OK* or press Enter.

Now display the codes once more by pressing Alt-F3 and remove the codes [HPg]. Place the cursor on the second blank line under the Report text section. Select *Layout, Tables, Create*. Specify **1** at Columns and click on *OK* or press Enter. Mark the text from the beginning of the **glass** text to the end. Select *Edit, Cut*. Activate the table frame by clicking in it or by moving to it with the cursor. Select *Edit, Paste*. The text is now in the frame. Select *File, Save As*. Enter **twinrep3**. Select *File, Close*.

12 Letters, reports, essays, posters

12.1 Letters on blank paper

Would you like to create your own style of letters although you do not have headed paper with your logo or name and address? You may require a printer which is capable of printing extra large letters using a large font or a scalable font (a font which can be enlarged or reduced). Additional software providing extra fonts is also a possibility (see chapter 15). If this is not the case, you may consider using the Windows printer driver instead of the WordPerfect driver. This enables you to print larger letters, although there is a risk that these may not be printed quite so neatly on the paper, or the process may be more time-consuming. (See also chapter 14 concerning the Windows printer driver.)

First determine whether you wish to adjust the margins. The default setting is 1" from the left- and right-hand edges of the paper while the distance from the top and bottom edges is also 1". Adjust the margins as required but keep in mind that that it is not pleasant reading if the margins are reduced to 0.5" and that most printers cannot print a letter well if the upper margin is too small. Adjustment of the margins takes place via the *Layout, Margins* menu.

Now determine which font you wish to use for your own (company) name, for other address data etc. and for the text in the letter. If the company is one which should exude a certain 'old-fashioned reliability', you could consider using a traditional font with serif, such as Times Roman, Dutch, Garamond or (New) Century Schoolbook. A company wishing to create a more modern impression may prefer a more rigid font without serif, such as Univers, Modern or Avant Garde. Helvetica (also known as Swiss) and Bookman are quite neutral. More elegant impression is made by Palatino (or its variant

Zapf Calligraphic), Garamond Italic and the Windows font Script. In addition, there are dozens of less common or fantasy fonts available as 'soft fonts'. Avoid fonts in your company name which strongly resemble normal typewriter letters, such as Courier, Line Printer, Pica and Brougham. (See also chapter 6 concerning fonts.)

When dealing with a company name, it is often convenient to have it at the top of (the first page of) the letter. Select a 24 or 30 point font size. In the case of a long name this should not be too large otherwise the name will not fit onto one line. If the font size is specified in cpi (characters per inch), try out 5, 6 or 7. Select bold and/or italics and centre the name on the page. If you prefer it, you can also have it right-aligned.
You can set the other data (address, telephone number, fax, bank account number) in a smaller font of the same type (e.g. 11 or 12 points, or 10 cpi) directly under the name or at the bottom of the page. If you also place the text at the top of the page, you can left-align it, or centre it under the name or indent it a little to the right using tabs. If you wish to place this data at the bottom, it can be useful to make a footer to do this (see chapter 7).

If you use a special letter for the company name, it may be advisable to use a more common and more legible font for the address data etc. Then you should use a font which corresponds as much as possible to the font used in the name, and which does not differ too much from the font which you are going to use in the letter itself. If you wish to use the same font in the letter as in the address data etc., you can produce a small distinction by using a bold version for the address data.

If the letter concerns personal correspondence, you can place your name and address in the top right-hand corner, as you normally would, in an 11 or 12 point size and in italics or bold if required. You can also place this text centred at the top of the page, but this is less common. You can also draw a thin line across the breadth of the page between your name and address and the rest of the letter.

In the case of personal correspondence, you can now select the font for the text of the letter and this can also be used for the name and address of the recipient, for the date and for the page numbering if applicable.

If you do not wish to have a number on the first page, you can switch off the numeration for the first page (see chapter 7).

If this is correspondence which involves a company, it may be desirable to place the company name at the top of all pages. Select the same font as at the beginning, perhaps a little smaller if you prefer. Centre it or right-align it just as you did on the first occasion.

Page numbering is recommended. Regarding the contents of the letter, select an easily read font without embellishment.

If you frequently write letters in this way, it can be extremely useful to create macros for these procedures. Then you can place your name and address data on a letter in the required font with the appropriate settings for the margins, page numbering etc.

In order to place the date in the letter, you can use the *date* function. There are two possibilities:

- The date as text. The date is registered in the document in the same way as specified now. You can enter the date using the *Tools, Date, Text* menu options.
- The date as code. Each time you retrieve a document, the valid date is entered. You can specify the date code using the Tools, Date, Code menu options.

If you wish to alter the way in which the date is specified, you can do this using the *Tools, Date, Format* menu options. Select *Edit Date Format* to select from the different options for the date format.

Consider whether the lines in the letter should be justified or not. If you do not alter the default setting, the *Justification* feature will be on, in other words, there is always a straight right-hand edge to the text. This means
that sometimes the spaces between the words are in-
creased in order to fill out the line. If you wish to change
this, switch the *Justification* off. Select *Layout, Justification, Full.* If there is no tick mark placed in front of this
option, no justification will take place.

12.2   Letters on headed paper

If the name and address of the sender are already
printed on the letter paper, it is advisable to select a font
which resembles the printed heading for the text of the
letter, unless you specially want to use a contrasting
font.

In any case, you will have to make allowances for what
is already printed. If there is a logo and/or text at the top
or bottom, you will have to measure the distance from
the top of the paper to the position where you can actually begin the letter. Specify this distance as the upper
margin (*Layout, Margins*). This also applies to the bottom margin.

If you are using window envelopes and the name and
address of the recipient has to fit exactly, this is a bit
more complicated. Use the Advance function (see
chapter 11).

Measure the distance from the left edge of the paper to
the position of the envelope window. If this is greater
than the left margin, alter the margin or use a tab (or
several tabs) at the beginning of each address line. If
you have shifted the margin, having typed the address,
reset the margin for the letter text.

Measure the distance from the top of the paper to the
position where the envelope window stops. Add half an
inch to this. Now move to the calculated position to
begin the letter text.

12.3 Invoices

The same rules apply to invoices as to letters concerning typing names, addresses etc. on blank or pre-printed paper. It is useful to make a table for the invoice data.

12.4 Invitations and posters

Of course, an invitation and a poster are not the same thing, but they do have common properties: they should both be conspicuous and there should not be too much text. The main information consists of: what (which event), when (date and time) and where (the place, with transport information if necessary). Other information should be restricted to indicating what makes it worthwhile to attend such an event. Sometimes one slogan is enough, or a line which arouses the curiosity of the reader.

Use your imagination to give it an original appearance. However, do not allow your fantasy to run riot: six different fonts, a page full of pictures or a text without (visible) structure tend to give a chaotic and thus unattractive impression. You do not have to show off to your friends and acquaintances what you are capable of doing with WordPerfect.

If your printer has the capacity, use a large font for the important information. Do not use more than one font in one line. Place an important section of text in a frame in order to emphasize it.

12.4.1 Invitations

A business invitation should have a firm appearance. Use a font without too much ornamentation which is easily legible. If the invitation comes from a business which sells a product which, in one way or another, can be associated with a certain font, you can have a section of the text printed using that font. In the case of a business which supplies products of a more artistic nature, it may be a good idea to use an ornate letter in some sections of the text.

A personal invitation to some good friends to a family party for example, can be given a familiar touch by choosing a pseudo-handwritten font (e.g. Script, if you are using the Windows printer driver).
Use a large font to make something conspicuous but do not exaggerate. Letters the size of a newspaper headline are not suitable for an invitation.

12.4.2   Posters

The layout of a good poster is not self-evident. Consider the following points carefully:

- What should appear in order to attract attention? A text or a picture?
- What is the most important information on the poster?
- What additional information is required?
- And also of great importance: what is *not* necessary?

When designing a poster, you should keep in mind that this should be conspicuous from a distance. Accordingly, ensure that the most important message is conveyed in large letters. Use a 48 point letter or larger. Restrict the rest of the text to a minimum. The really indispensable factors are the drawing of attention to the event, and essential data such as date, time and place. In general, the reader will not absorb a lengthy text. Nevertheless, if you consider a number of lines absolutely necessary, do not make these too large although they should be legible at a reasonable distance. Use a 24 to 30 points letter size for this.

When recommending letter sizes, we are taking the A4 page size as norm, since this is the format to which most laser and inkjet printers are geared. If you are able

to print a larger format, it is obvious that you can work
with larger letters.

12.5 Reports, essays, books

WPWin is a wonderful tool for making reports and essays. The functions dealt with in chapter 11, paragraph
numbering, table of contents and index can be em-
ployed here. Styles (as explained in chapter 9) and
headers and footers (chapter 7) can also be applied.

A facility which you probably wish to use is that of endnotes. You can quickly learn how this works using the
Layout, Endnote menu option. The available Options
are interesting: you can select special display of the
endnote numbers (superscript is the default setting),
you may use letters instead of numbers, you can number the endnotes according to the page or cumulatively
throughout the entire document, you can place them at
the end of the document instead of at the bottom of the
page etc. The *New Number* menu option enables you to
begin the numbering at number 1 each time you begin a
new chapter.

Here are some tips concerning layout:

- Reserve an entire page for the title and for other important information which you wish to register at the
  beginning of the document. Keep this as brief as
  possible.
- Begin the table of contents on a fresh page. Do the
  same for the text.
- Begin the index on a new page.
- If the text is divided into lengthy chapters, begin each
  chapter on a new page.
- Ensure sufficient space between the paragraphs.
  This makes the document more orderly and benefits
  the legibility.
- Type the text first, then place the codes for the table
  of contents, index, font etc. A text which already includes many codes is difficult to edit.

If you find that WPWin runs rather slowly on your computer, do not create a lengthy document in one go. Divide the text over various documents and only join these when it is time to generate the table of contents and the index.

13 Mailing, catalogues and dBase files

We shall deal with a number of interesting WordPerfect applications for the advanced user in this chapter. We shall discuss the merge feature in more depth and the corresponding subject of mailing. In addition, more information will be given concerning how data from dBase files can be used for merging in WordPerfect. Finally, we shall outline a possibility which you have perhaps not yet considered: creating a catalogue using data from a database and the Merge feature.

13.1 Mailing

If you wish to send letters with individual names and addresses, but having identical contents, to a number of connections or potential customers, you should use the **Merge** function. The actual letter only needs to be written once. Codes are placed where the name, address etc. are to be positioned. This letter is called the primary file in WordPerfect. The variable data are placed in a separate file: the name of the recipient, the address, postal code, town etc. This file is called the secondary file.

13.1.1 The letter and the address list

The letter, the *primary file*, is written in the normal way. You can see on the screen just how the letter will turn out on paper. Instead of the name, address etc. codes are placed at the corresponding positions. The number of codes needed depends on the variable data you wish to use and the number of *fields* making up your *secondary file*, the address list.

A field consists of one sort of information in a list containing the same type of data. For example, one field

contains the name of a person or a firm, another field
contains the street name and so forth. Each group of
data belonging together (in other words, data concerning one person or firm) is called a *record*. All records in
an address list should have the same structure.

An address list could look like this:

```
Ronald Duncie{END FIELD}
6, Priestess Rise{END FIELD}
Stonehenge SH1 7IB{END FIELD}
{END RECORD}
==========================================
Sheena O'Conan{END FIELD}
8 Pope Gardens{END FIELD}
Dublin DB4 2GP{END FIELD}
{END RECORD}
==========================================
Richard Cliff{END FIELD}
1 Hallelujah Lane{END FIELD}
London L12 5SP{END FIELD}
{END RECORD}
==========================================
```

You will notice:

- The name is always on the first line.
- The house number and street are always on the second line.
- A code has been placed at the end of each line {END
  FIELD}.
- A code has been placed at the end of each record
  {END RECORD}, followed by a Hard Page Return
  code. This is made by pressing Ctrl-Enter, but when-
  ever you enter an {END RECORD} code, a hard
  page code is automatically placed. A hard page
  break is displayed on the screen by a double line
  across the whole width of the document window.

How to place the codes has been dealt with in chapter
11.

The letter could look something like this:

```
{FIELD}1~
{FIELD}2~
{FIELD}3~


Dear Sir/Madam,

In the light of your recent concern about
the relative positions of science and
belief, and the position of mankind in the
universe, we are pleased to announce that
the honourable gentleman Mr. Galileo
Galilei has now been fully reinstated. In
fact, he was recently exhumed and we all
heartily shook his hand.

Yours faithfully,
J. Torquemada (Jr.)
```

When the merge function is used, a document is created consisting of the same amount of pages as there are records (3 in this case), with the text of the letter on each page, with a different name and address above each page.

13.1.2   Creating an address list

In order to make a letter a little more personal, you can also type an introduction for each letter and, if desired, a code for the signature. If you find it useful, you can also place other information in the address file, such as telephone numbers. The address can be saved as one unit, if required. Then you can only use an address in its entirety, but this way of working saves you having to insert one or more *end field* codes in each address, and it is also useful if the addresses do not all consist of the same number of lines.

First type a name:

```
P. Verboeven
```

Set an *End Field* code directly behind this (use Alt-Enter
or use a button on the button bar).
You move automatically to a new line. Now type the address, pressing Enter at the end of each line, except
after the postal code:

```
Blood View,
1, Basic St.,
Douglas DG1 2SS
```

Place an *End field* code directly behind the postal code.
Now enter the introduction to the letter:

```
Dear Paul,
```

Place an *End field* code directly after the comma. Now
type an abbreviation for the conclusion of the letter:

```
yrsn
```

Place an *End record* code here. After this code, a hard
page break is made automatically.
Create the following records in the same way:

```
A. Hitchkick{END FIELD}
43 Vertigo Heights
Tomintoul TM1 2NB{END FIELD}
Dear Alfred,{END FIELD}
yrsn{END FIELD}
{END RECORD}
============================================
E. Scoda{END FIELD}
400 Brute Hill
Rome SC9 1BW
Italy{END FIELD}
Dear Mister Scoda,{END FIELD}
yrf{END FIELD}
{END RECORD}
============================================
```

```
Silver Screen Curtains Ltd.
Ms. M. Bunroe{END FIELD}
2 Kennedy Lane
TR5 2BT Tralee{END FIELD}
Dear Ms. Bunroe,{END FIELD}
wwg{END FIELD}
{END RECORD}
============================================
```

You can add more records yourself. Keep in mind that the structure remains the same:

- the name is always in the first field,
- the complete address in the second field,
- the complete introduction in the third field,
- an abbreviation for the conclusion in the fourth field. Do not use abbreviations other than **yrsn, yrf and wwg**.

Save the file as ADDRESS.LST or under a name of your choice and clear the screen.

13.1.3 Creating a form letter

We shall now examine how a letter is made using these data. First place the codes for the name and address at the top of the letter. Press Enter three times in order to create two blank lines. Now enter the date. Press Enter twice to skip a line. Now place the code for the introduction. This is the third field.
Press Enter twice and type the first paragraph:

```
Thank you for your interest in our course
Learning to make your own video. The response
was enormous, exceeding all expectations and
this has forced us to make a selection out of
the (more than fifty!) candidates.
Unfortunately, you have not been chosen,
although the selection committee did register
good points in the work you sent to us. Lack
of experience and talent were the main
reasons given.
```

```
Nevertheless, your personal data have been
archived and we hope to offer you a place in
one of our courses in the future. Don't give
up. Remember, 90% of inspiration is
perspiration!
On behalf of the Arts Council:
```

Press Enter twice and enter the code for the fourth field, which contains an abbreviation for the conclusion of the letter.

Formulate the letter further as you wish. Save the letter as LETTER.MRG or under another name of your choice. Clear the screen.

It is now time to merge the letter and the address list. Select *Tools, Merge, Merge.*
A new file has been created, consisting of the same amount of pages as there are addresses. Go to the beginning of this document. Using the *Replace* function, you can now replace the abbreviations with complete conclusions:

- replace yrsn with: Yours sincerely,
- replace yrf with: Yours faithfully,
- replace wwg with: With warmest greetings,

You can now print the letters. If you wish to check that the letters are actually printed out as you want, print one letter first, in other words, one page of the file. If you are not satisfied, the best thing to do is alter the primary file (LETTER.MRG in the above example) and merge it with the address list once more. In general, this will absorb less time than adjusting each letter individually.

13.1.4   Empty fields for missing data

If the amount of data is not identical for each field, you must be alert to ensure the layout of the records remains the same. If this is not the case, your letter structure will go wrong. For example, if a field is reserved for telephone numbers and you do not know the number of someone in your address list, do not place text in the corresponding line. You should only specify the code {END FIELD}. In cases where empty fields occur, it is more convenient to use field names instead of field 1, field 2 etc. See Chapter 11.

13.2 Mailing addresses from a spreadsheet or database

If you have a list of addresses in a spreadsheet or database, it it a bit laborious to type this over into WordPerfect. This is (generally) unnecessary. In many cases, it is possible to convert these files, or the data you wish to extract from them, to a file which can be used as a secondary merge file in WordPerfect, although this may require a little adjustment. As an example, we shall convert dBase files which are the most widely-used form of data file on the PC, since not only dBase lll and dBase IV use this file format, but also various other programs which work with databases also use it.

13.3 dBase/Foxbase/Clipper files

We shall assume that there is a file called CON-NECTS.DBF in which the following fields exist:

```
CONNECTNR      POSTADD      CONTACTPERS
SEARCHCODE     TOWN         TO:
FIRMNAME       POSTCODE     INTRO
FIRMADD        POSTLAND     BANKNR
FIRMTOWN       TEL          [etc.]
FIRMPCODE      TELEX
FIRMLAND       TELEFAX
```

There will be many more fields but we shall presume that they are not important at this moment. The fields we need now are: FIRMNAME, TO:, POSTADD, TOWN, POST-CODE, POSTLAND, INTRO.

Since the fields containing the address and postal code must be able to contain letters and numbers, we shall presume in this case that all the relevant fields are character fields.

13.3.1   Converting files in dBase/Foxbase

We shall convert the relevant fields to a file which can be processed by WordPerfect. We presume that the files used in WordPerfect are stored in the directory C:WPFILE. The new file will also be placed in this directory. All the relevant fields, when the CONNECTS file is in use, are copied to this directory by typing the following command at the dBase or Foxbase prompt. Type the command on one line:

```
copy to c:\wpfile\address fields firmname,
to:, postadd, town, postcode, postland, intro
delimited.
```

If everything has gone smoothly, the message appears

```
22 records copied
```

(or perhaps another number than 22, depending on the size of the file). The address file created in the C:\WPFILE directory is now called ADDRESS.TXT. The .TXT extension has been added by dBase or Foxbase automatically. You can now leave dBase or Foxbase using **quit**.

If you work with Clipper, a program will have to be made to implement what we have just described. Of course, this can be programmed in dBase or Foxbase, so that a selection based on certain criteria can be made from the entire file. Further processing in WordPerfect takes place as outlined above.

13.3.2   The letter

When typing the letter, we should keep a number of factors in mind. First, pay attention to the order of sequence of the fields when they have been converted from the dBase file. FIRMNAME becomes Field 1, POSTADD becomes Field 2 etc. Town and postal code belong together. Accordingly, place these adjacent to one another on the same line with two spaces between them. The introduction may not have a comma in the dBase file, otherwise the merging will not be executed properly.

Therefore, you should place a comma in the letter itself. The letter should look something like this:

```
{FIELD}1~
{FIELD}2~
{FIELD}3~  {FIELD}4~
{FIELD}5~

{FIELD}6~


London, 10th of January 1993


{FIELD}7~,
```

A new year has just begun and this is the time to make a fresh start with original creative ideas. We have a number of up-and-coming young film-makers in our files and in the light of the Government cut-backs in public spending, we wish to introduce this young talent to the commercial sector. The enclosed catalogue gives an impression of the avant-garde approach.

If you are considering making a small promotional film for your company or any kind of advertising campaign, the unbridled imagination of this new, young talent is

```
indispensable. In addition, you may be sure
that they will work their fingers to the
bone for almost nothing.
A copy of our fees is included at the end
of the catalogue.

Yours sincerely,

The Arts Council Job Agency.
```

Save this letter as ARTSCNL.LET and clear the screen (*Close*).

13.3.3   Merging the files

We shall now merge the ARTSCNL.LET and the AD-DRESS.TXT files. Begin with an empty screen (new document). Select *Tools, Merge, Merge*. Specify **artscnl.let** as the primary file and move the cursor to the second text box, using the mouse or by pressing Tab. Place a cross in the *ASCII Delimited Text* box using the mouse or by pressing the spacebar. Click on *OK* or press Enter.

You must now specify which separators are to be used. When converting dBase files to .TXT files a comma is placed **behind** each field in a record. After each record, a *carriage return* and a *line feed* are placed to ensure that the next record begins on a new line. WordPerfect has already specified that there is no separator at the beginning of a field and a comma at the end of a field. This is how it should be, therefore you do not need to make any alterations. If record separators have already been entered: nothing at the beginning, a [CR], in other words, a *carriage return* at the end of each record, yet another code must be specified. Position the cursor behind the [CR] code, activate the button next to the text box, select *Line Feed* and the code [LF] will be placed behind the code [CR]. Now click on *OK* or press Enter.

13.3.4   Completing the mailing

If you examine the letters, you will observe that the name
of a country is registered under the address. Great Britain repeatedly recurs although the letter is sent in Great
Britain. If you wish to remove superfluous country names
from the address list, proceed as follows. Go to the begining of the file and replace the words *Great Britain* with
nothing (using *Edit, Replace*). By using the search function to find the words *Great Britain*, they will always be
found.
Your letter is now ready to be printed.

13.4   A catalogue from a database

If you have to make a catalogue from time to time, it can
be useful to save the data in a database. In principle,
you only need to do the following:

1. Make, using WordPerfect, a title sheet or initial text,
    a standard layout (page format, headers, footers)
    for the actual pages of the catalogue and a con-
    cluding page or end text.

2. Using WordPerfect, create a primary file in which
    the layout is established for one work or article in
    the catalogue (corresponding with one record in the
    database). The number of fields in the merge file
    must correspond with the number of fields in the
    database file.

3. Create a database structure which corresponds to
    the structure of the primary file. You may use any
    database in which the files, either directly or after
    conversion, can be used as secondary files in
    WordPerfect. For example, DataPerfect, dBase,
    Foxbase. The more primitive database, the Card
    Index supplied with Windows, cannot be used for
    this function. You may also use a spreadsheet,
    PlanPerfect or Lotus 1-2-3 for example, but then a
    number of possibilities provided by database pro-

grams are not available. You can now enter the
data for the work or article in the database.

4.   Alterations to the data can be easily made in the
     database. If you include fields containing certain
     codes in addition to the fields necessary to print the
     catalogue, you can easily alter groups of data si-
     multaneously. If, for example, the fees of one of
     your free-lancers are increased by 5%, and there is
     a field containing a free-lance code in the database,
     you can alter the fees in all records containing the
     relevant free-lance code by multiplying one order
     by 1.05.

5.   In order to create the catalogue, you only need to
     merge the primary file and the file from the data-
     base and replace the hard page breaks with noth-
     ing or a blank line. Then add this file to the file con-
     taining the title page and the general layout and
     supplement this with the end text.

13.4.1   Initial text and total layout

The title and other introductory remarks may be created
to suit your own requirements. Place the headers and
footers for the subsequent pages also in this file. As an
example, we shall choose a advertising agency sup-
plying promotional films. From time to time a new catalogue is composed, outlining various possibilities. In addition, potential customers should be able to gain more
detailed information regarding quality and reproduction.

We shall imagine we are going to create a rather extensive catalogue. A title page is required. The word
CATALOGUE will be placed there, the name and address of the agency and registration of the type of product dealt with. First make a sketch of the title page (see
figure).

Select a font for the title page.

Calculate the distance between the top of the paper and the word *CATALOGUE*. For example, the top of the first letter C should be placed 2.5" from the top edge. We shall now place the words **Catalogue, audio, video** at the appropriate position using the *Layout, Advance, To Position* menu options. Centre these words, make them bold and extra large.

Now specify where the name and address should be placed. That is approximately 9" from the top of the paper. Specify this position using the *To Position* option, place the name, address, town and postal code, and telephone number under one another.

We shall now select a font for the actual catalogue text. This can be the font already used but in a different size,

for instance 10 or 11 points. It may, of course be another type.

Now specify what should be placed at the top and bottom of the following pages. A header or a footer may
suffice, in which the agency name, the word CATA-
LOGUE and the page number are registered. The basis
has now been made. Save this file as TITLE.CAT.

13.4.2   Catalogue contents

Create a primary file for the data concerning one product.
This should look something like this:

Name of the product
Description of the product, several lines long if required.
Reference number:00000*Price*: £000.00

Of course, other numbers will be placed instead of
zeros. The primary file is created as follows:

```
--------------------------------------------------
{FIELD}1~
{FIELD}2~
Ref.nr.:{FIELD}3~Price: £{FIELD}4~
--------------------------------------------------------------------------
```

If everything has gone smoothly, the codes [Bold On]
and [Bold Off] will have been placed for {FIELD}1~ and
a code for [Tab] before the word Price in italics. Check
this via the code display, Alt-F3. Save the contents as
CONTENT.CAT.

13.4.3   Composing the catalogue

The file containing the catalogue must now be converted to a .TXT file in the same way as the form letters
described above. Merge the .TXT file as the secondary
file with the CONTENT.CAT file which now serves as
the primary file. Use the *Edit, Replace, Codes* function

to replace the [HPg] code with the code [HRt] twice.
Save the merged file as CATAL.MRG.
Now retrieve the TITLE.CAT file, place the cursor at the
end of this file, retrieve CATAL.MRG, add a concluding
text and the new catalogue is completed. If necessary,
improve the layout through the various pages.

Exercises

1. Create a secondary merge file. Name the fields:
    Name, Address, PCode, Town. Then make up
    some names and addresses. Create at least two
    records. Assign the name NAMES to the file.

2. Create a primary merge file. It should look some-
    thing like this:

```
{FIELD}name~
{FIELD}address~
{FIELD}town~ {FIELD}pcode~

Dear Sir/Madam,
As you know, a number of prisons will
shortly be privatized. Shares in these
ventures will shortly be coming on the
market. This promises to be a booming
industry with a growth rate which has
not been achieved since the industrial
revolution. Take your chance and
subscribe now. You can also ensure
success by becoming a criminal
yourself. Please find enclosed one
crowbar and one mask.

Yours faithfully,
Michael Hellestein.

P.S. If you don't pay, the bailiff will
be sent.
```

Save the file under the name SHARES.

3.   Merge the NAMES and SHARES files.

Procedures

1.   Select *Tools, Merge, Merge Codes*. Use the Cursor
     Down key to move through the list until you have
     found Field Names. Highlight this and select *Insert*.
     Specify **name** for Field 1. Press Alt-A (for Add)).
     Specify **address** for Field 2. Press Alt-A. Specify
     town for Field 3. Press Alt-A. Specify **pcode** for
     Field 4. Press Enter.
     You can now enter the data for the first field. The
     field in which you are currently working is displayed
     at the bottom of the screen. After specifying each
     field, select *Tools, Merge, End Field*, except after
     the postal code when you should select *Tools,
     Merge, End Record*. When several records have
     been created, select *File, Save As* and assign the
     name NAMES. Select *File Close*.

2.   Select *Tools, Merge, Field*. Type **name** and click on
     OK or press Enter. Then press Enter. Select *Tools,
     Merge, Field*. Type **address** and click on *OK* or
     press Enter. Press Enter. Select *Tools, Merge,
     Field*. Type **town** and click on *OK* or press Enter.
     Press the spacebar twice. Select *Tools, Merge,
     Field*. Type **pcode** and click on *OK* or press Enter.
     Then press Enter. Type the rest of the letter. Select
     File, Save As. Specify SHARES and select *File,
     Close*.

3.   Select *Tools, Merge, Merge*. Specify **names** as the
     primary file and **shares** as the secondary file. Click
     on *OK* or press Enter.

14   Printing

14.1   Choosing the printer driver

During the installation of WPWin you were able to spec-ify whether you also wanted to have the WordPerfect printer driver installed or only the Windows printer driver. Hopefully you selected a WP printer driver for one or more printers; if not, it is still possible to do this. What are the advantages of the WordPerfect printer driver over the standard printer driver used by Win-dows? The answer lies in the print quality and in the printing speed. As long as you only make use of the de-fault fonts in your printer, there will be little difference in the quality of your printouts. However, when dealing with special characters, such as ô, ò, Γ and π, a clear distinction can be made. Using Windows, some charac-ters will just not be printed, and sometimes you will get other characters on paper than you had on the screen. Certain graphical symbols are reproduced broadly and raggedly by Windows in comparison to others. In general, WordPerfect prints quicker using its own WP printer driver than using the Windows Print Manager.

Nevertheless, the Windows printer driver does also have its benefits, especially if you are using a printer which normally does not print large letters. Windows is capable of printing 14, 18 and 24 point letters using any printer. In this case, you must make use of the Modern or Roman fonts from Windows. In addition, there are programs on the market which improve the print quality of Windows. This is dealt with in more detail in the fol-lowing chapter.

14.2   Selecting a printer

If more than one printer driver has been installed, you must make a choice. This should be done preferably when you begin a new document. Accordingly, you can keep the capabilities of the printer in mind. How do you select another printer?

M   Click on *File, Select Printer*. The current printer is shown in the Select Printer box which then appears. In addition the connection to the computer is also registered along with the printer driver used (WordPerfect or Windows). In the lower part of this box, you are able to choose from the printer driver programs from WordPerfect and Windows. Click on the printer driver of your choice. The names of printers for which the chosen driver is suitable appear in a window. Double click on the appropriate printer.

K   Press Alt-F, and type an L. The current printer will be displayed at the top of the Printer Select box, along with the registration of the connection to the computer and the printer driver used (WordPerfect or Windows). You can select the printer driver programs from WordPerfect or Windows in the lower part of the window. Press Alt-W to select the WordPerfect driver or Alt-N for the Windows driver. The names of the printers for which the chosen driver is suitable appear in a window. Press Alt-V to move to this window. Choose a printer using Cursor Up or cursor down and press Enter.

14.3   Printer setup

Using the window mentioned above, you can also adjust the default printer settings. Select *Setup* and the Printer Setup dialogue box appears. There are three text boxes in this window. The name of the printer is shown in the upper box. You can specify another name here if that helps you to distinguish between various printers or printer connections.

A second text box enables you to specify where the *downloadable* fonts and printer commands are located. There are printers which are capable of printing other fonts than the built-in ones if you supply the necessary information concerning these fonts from the computer. This is called 'downloading'.

Subsequently, you can specify the initial font. This is the font with which WordPerfect will begin working when you begin a new document while this printer has been selected. Click on *Initial Font* or press Alt-F. A window appears containing the fonts with which we are familiar from chapter 6. Double click on the name of the required font, or use the Cursor Up or Cursor Down key to highlight the font and then press Enter.

If you use a sheet feeder, click on *Sheet Feeder* or press Alt-S in order to specify the type.

The connection is important. Is the printer connected to the first parallel port (LPT1) as usual? Click on *Port* or press Alt-P to choose between the serial and the parallel ports or to select printing to a file. If you select printing to a file, you can specify a file name under a directory in the window.

If you are working with a network, the chosen printer could be a network printer. If that is the case, click on the option button for Network Printer or press Alt-E. You can remove the cross again by repeating the procedure.

If you use a printer with font cartridges, click on *Cartridges/Fonts* or press Alt-C to specify those you wish to use.

14.4   Windows printer setup

The settings for Windows printers can also be altered via Setup, but this procedure produces a completely different dialogue box. In the upper part, you can select another printer. Under this, there are options dealing with paper supply and paper size. In addition, you may choose between the print settings *Portrait* which is the normal setting, or *Landscape*. The latter is not available on every printer and even then not with every font.

The graphic resolution can be set to 75, 150, 300 or even 600 dpi (dots per inch) (Options/Advanced). A higher resolution increases the image quality but also the printing time. You can specify a default number of copies and select cartridge fonts if applicable. By selecting *Fonts*, you can install *soft fonts* or *downloadable fonts* which are sent to the printer using the appropriate software.

14.5 Specifying the paper size

Specification of the paper size is necessary when you use a size other than A4 (8.27" by 11.69"). Do this directly at the beginning of your document.

M   Click on *Layout, Page, Paper Size*. A window appears showing various paper sizes. By clicking on the arrows in the scroll bar, you can move through the list. Double click on an option in order to select it. Click on *Add* in order to define a paper size which does not appear in the list.

K   Press Alt-F9, then S. A window appears showing various paper sizes. Pressing Cursor Down enables you to move through the list. Press Alt-A to specify a paper size which does not appear in the list. Press Alt-S to select the highlighted format from the list.

If you wish to permanently use a paper size other than A4, alter the default setting in WordPerfect. Select *File, Preferences, Initial Codes*. Remove the first code ([Paper Sz/Typ:8.27" x 11.69",Standard]). Select a format in the way outlined above. Click on *Close* or press Alt-C.

14.6   Installing new WordPerfect printers

Do you wish to install a new printer in WPwin?

M   Click on *File, Select Printer, Add*. First look through the list which now appears on the screen to see if the relevant printer is registered. If so, click on the file name (or highlight the file name and press Enter). Click on *OK* or press Enter and click on *Select* if required.

K   Press Alt-F, then L and then Alt-A. Look through the list which now appears on the screen to see if the relevant printer is registered. If so, highlight it using the Cursor Down key, press Enter, and press Enter once again. If you wish to select this printer as the default printer, press Enter yet again, otherwise press Esc.

If the new printer is not included in the list shown, proceed as follows from the moment that you notice this. Press Esc twice, press Alt-F4 to quit WordPerfect and press Alt-F4 again to quit Windows.
Now go to the directory in which the WPWin program files are located. Normally you will give the command

```
cd \wpwin
```

to do this.
Now type

```
install
```

and press Enter. Continue by specifying Y(es), 4 (printer), a: or b: (depending on the size of your Word-Perfect diskettes). Ensure that the Printer 1 diskette is located in the appropriate drive and make a selection by moving through the list using Cursor Down and typing the letter which is located in front of the printer name. Respond Y(es), and Y again if you wish to install more printers. Press Esc to conclude the installation. Activate Windows once again, activate WordPerfect again, select the printer which has just been added to the list if you wish to use it immediately.

14.7   Installing new Windows printers

In order to do this, you must have the Windows diskettes available, unless the printer in question is one which
uses the printer driver of a printer which has already
been installed. Quit WordPerfect. Activate the Main
Group window by clicking on the title bar or by pressing
Ctrl-Tab as many times as is necessary. Select *Control
Panel* then *Printers*. Select *Add*. Look for the required
printer using the Cursor Down key. Double click on the
printer name or press Enter when the name is highlighted. In many cases, Windows will request a diskette.
Insert the required diskette in drive A: and click on *OK*
or press Enter. If the diskette must be inserted in B:,
alter the A:\ in the window to B:\.

Note: Be alert to the fact that when carrying out a later
installation, Windows may make an error in the diskette
numbering. If, for instance, diskette nr.6 is requested
and this is rejected, try nr.7 or nr.5.

The name of the printer appears in the Installed Printers
window along with the message 'None, Inactive'. Click
on *Connect* or press Alt-C. Use Cursor Down to move
to the port to which the printer is or will be connected
(mainly LTP1:). Click on *Settings* or press Alt-S. Specify
the paper size and click on *OK* or press Enter twice. If
you wish to use the newly installed printer directly, click
on *Setup*, or press Alt-S and then cursor up. Click on
OK or press Enter.
You are now able to use this printer in WordPerfect
when you select the Windows printer driver.

14.8   Print preview

Before having something printed, you can use the Print
Preview to check if it is going to appear on paper as you
actually want. Although WPWin provides the *WYS-
IWYG* (*what you see is what you get*)option, the small
defects in the Windows system result in the letters
being reproduced imperfectly on the screen, and re-

viewing a whole page at once is not possible unless you have an A4 screen.

Requesting a print preview is easily done:

M   Click on *File, Print Preview*. You can examine a whole page by clicking on *Pages, Full Page*. If you wish to see everything in (more than) real size, click on *View, 100%*. Select *View, Zoom In* if you wish to see an enlarged version, or *View, Zoom Out* if you wish to reduce the document (and thus, show more of it on the screen). Options like *200%* and *Facing Pages* from the *Pages* menu are self-explanatory. If you wish to print something, select *File, Print*. If you wish to continue editing or to begin a new document, select *File, Close*.

K   Press Shift-F5. Using Alt-V and Alt-P, you are able to choose from a great number of options, such as viewing a whole page, in and out zooming, enlarging to 200% or viewing 2 facing pages. You can begin printing by pressing F5. You return to the document by pressing Ctrl-F4.

D   Press Alt-Shift-F7. See above concerning the many self-evident options. Press Shift-F7 to start printing. Press F7 to return to the document.

14.9   Printing

Do you wish to print a whole or part of a document?

M   Click on *File*, then on *Print*. If you just wish to print the entire document once, *Print* is sufficient.

K   Press F5. If you only wish to print the entire document once, press Enter.

D   Press Shift-F7. If you only wish to print the entire document once, press Enter.

However, there are more possibilities available. You can choose another printer using *Select*. The Print options are self-explanatory. Remember, if you choose *Current Page*, the page in which the cursor is currently located will be printed. You can increase the number of copies and you can specify whether the printer or Word-Perfect should do this. If paper has to be bound, you can specify a binding offset.

You can specify the graphics quality and the text quality. In both cases, you may choose between *High, Medium, Draft* and *Do Not Print*. The last option is only meaningful if you only wish to see a part of the document on the screen. In the case of text quality, *Draft* provides a low quality, but rapid printout. This difference is only noticeable on matrix and inkjet printers.
There is no difference on laser printers when dealing with text quality, but there is a difference with graphic quality. Keep in mind the various foreign characters and graphic symbols which may be graphically printed. The difference in quality is clear in these cases, and even more so with pictures.

15 Getting more out of your printer

In this chapter, we shall examine whether you can perhaps get more out of your printer than the standard
possibilities provide. WordPerfect and Windows already
assist in doing this. If you are willing to invest in extension in one form or another, much more is possible. By
extension, we mean additions to the printer itself or
extra software.

15.1 Optimal results with WordPerfect and Windows

The WordPerfect printer driver program for your printer
is probably the best there is. WordPerfect utilizes all
fonts and supports all specific possibilities of your
printer. Letters with which the printer is unfamiliar are
printed graphically. Images are also printed perfectly, at
least, if you have set the graphics quality to High.

Windows has geared the printer driver to each individual printer to a lesser extent than WordPerfect. Nevertheless, it provides other interesting facilities: use of the
Windows (3.0) fonts, such as Modern (a thin font without serif), Roman (a classical font) and Script (resem-
bling written text). All three are available in point sizes
from 6 to 48, but are printed a little raggedly from size
24 upwards. A 24 point font size will generally suffice.

15.2 Improving the Windows print quality

If you wish to print using Windows, first check whether
your printer resolution is set to the highest possible
value. In the case of laser printers, that is mostly 300 x
300 dpi.

There are various programs available with which you can improve the Windows print quality, although with the TrueType fonts of version 3.1 few people will find the need to do so. Adobe Type Manager is the most well-known of these. This not only provides additional fonts which can be used on any printer in a better quality than Windows version 3.0 can normally reproduce, it also ensures that the letters are displayed more clearly on the screen, i.e. the screen display corresponds better to the result on paper. Type Manager can be purchased separately, but is also supplied along with other packages, such as PageMaker and Ami Pro.

15.3   Extending the printer

Cartridges with additional fonts are available for diverse printers, especially laser printers and inkjet printers. In order to be able to use these fonts, an extension to the printer memory is required in many cases, in addition to the cartridge containing the fonts. This can be an expensive business. Nevertheless, for many users, this is an attractive way of getting precisely that font which they are eager to use on the printer. Purchasing a new printer is a more expensive solution.

One option for most laser printers is the extension to PostScript. PostScript provides approximately 35 sets of fonts, continuously scalable, allowing the user to print illustrations of a higher quality than normal: black areas are evenly black, various grey tints are clearly distinguishable. A disadvantage of working with PostScript cartridges is that printing can be quite time-consuming. In addition, the PostScript cartridges are rather expensive and generally require an extension of the printer memory. When purchasing a new printer, it is advisable to select one which is already equipped with PostScript.

15.4   Adding fonts via software

There are programs available for installing other fonts in
a printer. These are mostly less expensive than a cartridge, but working with *downloadable* fonts frequently
requires extending the printer memory. However, there
are programs which do not demand this.

15.5   Software emulation of PostScript

PostScript is really a printer language. The printer receives instructions in a special program language, inter-
prets these and prints the result. It is possible to allow
the interpretation process to be done by the computer
instead of by the printer. The computer converts the information to graphic information for the printer.
This can be done using a graphic card for the PC, which
is a rather expensive but quick solution, or by using software specially created for this purpose. This latter option is substantially less expensive, but printing takes
longer. The time consumed depends on the computer
speed, the presence or absence of EMS memory and
the availability of a co-processor. Several minutes per
page on a 386 computer is not exceptional.

If you wish to work with this kind of program, you should
install an Apple Laserwriter printer in WordPerfect or
Windows and give the instruction to print to a file. Printing via WordPerfect seems to produce the best results
here. To specify the settings for a WordPerfect printer,
proceed as follows: select *File, Select Printer*. Highlight
the Apple Laserwriter, select *Setup*. Select *Port* and
subsequently choose *File*. Specify the directory and file
name of your choice, for example, c:\print\wp.ps. Click
on *OK* or press Enter, twice. Keep in mind that you can
only print once in each WP session unless you alter the
name of the file in the meantime.

Appendix A
ASCII/ANSI characters in
WordPerfect

Below is a list of characters in the ASCII and ANSI character sets which are not available on the keyboard.
These characters can be obtained in WordPerfect for
Windows by pressing the Alt key and the numbers on
the numeric keypad when NumLock has been switched
on.

127	⌂	156	£
128	Ç	157	¥
129	ü	158	₧
130	é	159	ƒ
131	â	160	á
132	ä	161	í
133	à	162	ó
134	å	163	ú
135	ç	164	ñ
136	ê	165	Ñ
137	ë	166	ª
138	è	167	º
139	ï	168	¿
140	î	169	⌐
141	ì	170	¬
142	Ä	171	½
143	Å	172	¼
144	É	173	¡
145	æ	174	«
146	Æ	175	»
147	ô		
148	ö		
149	ò		
150	û		
151	ù		
152	ÿ		
153	Ö		
154	Ü		
155	¢		

Appendix B
Your computer, Windows and WordPerfect

Whether you are able to use WordPerfect for Windows on your computer or not depends on the configuration of your computer. In addition to a suitable computer, you also require Windows version 3.0 or a more recent version. As far as the computer goes, there are two important factors: the processor and the internal memory.

The processor

The processor in the PC regulates the processing of the commands, the calculation and the internal operation of the data flow. Most computers have a processor with the type numbers 8088, 8086, 80286, 80386 or 80486. This is (generally) the order of rapidity. In the '386 and '486 types there are also SX and DX versions. The SX version is slower than the DX.

PCs with an 8088 or 8086 processor are referred to as XT. These are **not** suitable for WordPerfect for Windows. You can run WordPerfect or LetterPerfect on them and files which are created using WordPerfect for Windows or WordPerfect 5.1 or LetterPerfect are mutually interchangeable.

PCs with an 80286 processor are referred to as AT. For the moment, we shall refer to all computers with a higher or more advanced processor as 386 PCs, since the procedure in Windows using 386 and 486 computers is identical.

The memory

MS-DOS, the PC operating system, distinguishes between various sorts of memory:

■ basic memory (also referred to as conventional memory) and two types of extended memory:
■ *extended memory* and
■ *expanded memory*.

With most computers, the basic memory is 640 Kb (kilo-
bytes). This is sometimes 512 Kb, but that is too little to
work with Windows.

Extended memory exists only on ATs and 386 systems,
not on XTs. The size of the extended memory can vary
from 256 Kb to more than 15 Mb (megabytes). 1 Megabyte = 1024 Kb. In order to be able to work with Word-
Perfect for Windows, at least 1 Mb extended memory is
required (i.e. 2 Mb in total), but 3 Mb extended memory
(4 Mb in total) is recommended.

Expanded memory can be added to any PC. The size
may vary from 512 Kb to several Mb. The DOS versions
of WordPerfect make use of expanded memory, where-
as Windows does not. If your PC has expanded memory and you wish to use WordPerfect for Windows, find
out if the *expanded memory* can be changed into *extended memory*.

These three different sorts of memory are referred to as
the internal memory or RAM (*random access memory*).
This means the memory which is directly accessible to
the processor (in contrast to external memory on disk
etc.).

Windows modes

Windows 3.1 can operate in two modes: *standard mode*
and *enhanced mode*. Enhanced mode is often referred
to as '386 enhanced mode' because it only runs under a

'386 or higher processor. The possibilities in Windows vary according to the mode.

Standard mode is regarded as the normal mode by the creators of Windows. This mode is suitable for ATs with at least 1 Mb memory (640 basic and 256 or more extended; at least 1 Mb extended is required for WPWin) and for 386 PCs with less than 2 Mb (although less than 2 Mb is insufficient for WPWin). In standard mode, it is possible to switch back and forth between various applications including non-Windows programs. If no start options are specified when Windows is started up, Windows will run in standard mode on an AT computer unless too much memory is already occupied.

Windows will be started up in standard mode on a 386 if there is less than 1 Mb extended memory, and in *enhanced* mode if there is more than 1 Mb extended memory. In *enhanced* mode, you can work *simultaneously* with various non-Windows applications. In addition, Windows is then capable of using so-called *virtual memory*, which means that a part of the harddisk is temporarily used as extension of the internal memory (RAM).
Exceptions are:
By using the option **/3**, you can run Windows in enhanced mode on a 386 computer which has more than 384 Kb but less than 1 Mb extended memory. There is a strong likelihood that Windows will run slower than in standard mode which is the normal mode on a 386 PC with so little extended memory, but at least you can work with WordPerfect under Windows.

Normally Windows would work in enhanced mode on a 386 computer with more than 1 Mb extended memory. If you **exclusively** use Windows applications (programs which have been specially developed for Windows, such as WordPerfect for Windows), Windows runs quicker in standard mode. You can start up Windows in standard mode using the **/s** option.

The mouse

There is a distinction between the Microsoft type of mouse and the PC Systems mouse. In general, mice from other manufacturers are compatible with those from Microsoft or PC Systems or both. This can often be regulated by turning a switch. When working with Windows, almost any computer mouse is suitable. A Microsoft-compatible or a PS/2 mouse is always suitable. Of the two or three buttons on the mouse, the left is the most commonly used and sometimes the right-hand button is also in use.

You can work without a mouse, but this can be laborious in many situations. Moreover, a number of convenient options will not be available in WordPerfect for Windows without a mouse. A simple mouse, costing no more than £20 is sufficient. In addition, if you wish to work with graphic or DTP programs, a mouse is essential.

The screen

Windows will run well using most common monitors and video cards. The best results are achieved with a VGA card and a VGA screen with a high resolution.

If the PC has a LCD monitor, as is often the case with laptop and notebook computers, you may be able to make the screen display a bit clearer by specifying *inverse* video display, i.e. white on a black background instead of black on a white background.

In addition to LCD screens, plasma screens are often used in portable computers. The text file READ.ME, supplied along with Windows 3.0 and 3.1 (in the Windows directory) contains instructions for the necessary adjustments of the display colours in a Toshiba VGA compatible plasma screen.

Appendix C
Installing Windows

The Setup installation program is so well-constructed that it is unnecessary to deal with it extensively. Keeping the following supplementary remarks in mind, installation should be no problem.

■ Installation can only take place on a computer with a harddisk. There must be a minimum of 6 Mb available on harddisk but 8 Mb is recommended. For the enhanced mode, 10Mb is best.

■ If you have a mouse, it is advisable to connect it before installation, owing to the fact that Windows is already being started up during the installation.

■ Place disk nr. 1 in the chosen drive, switch to this drive by typing A: or B: and give the SETUP command.

■ Subsequently, you will be given the choice between *Express Setup* and *Custom Setup*. It is advisable to choose the first option. Choose *Custom Setup* only when you are reasonably familiar with basic principles of Windows. In the first case, almost everything will take place automaticaliy, in the second case, you must specify certain points. No accidents will occur, in the case of *Custom Setup*, if you follow the instructions which appear on the screen.

■ SETUP will check the hardware present during the installation (the graphic card, network etc.). When using *Custom Setup*, check if this information is correct.

■ Read the instructions given by SETUP carefully and follow them precisely.

If, in retrospect, it is obvious that you have missed something, you can use *Windows Setup* from Main to make additions or alterations without having to install Windows all over again.

This may apply, for example, to the keyboard layout which Setup may install to a setting other than the one

you wish. This layout, by the way, can be altered in the
Control Panel, using the *International* option (Keyboard
Layout).

Note: Do not attempt to copy the files directly from the
         disks to the harddisk. They are compressed
         and, therefore, have to be expanded before they
         are available as working programs. If, neverthe-
         less, it is necessary to work without using Setup,
         proceed as follows:

■ Copy EXPAND.EXE from disk nr. 3 to the harddisk.
   This program converts compressed files into working
   programs.
■ Place the source disk in one of the drives.
■ Give the following command, followed by Enter:

```
EXPAND A:file name C:file name
```

In this case, A: is the source drive (may also be B:) and
C: is the harddisk to which the files are being copied.
The files are copied to the harddisk and expanded.

Appendix D
Working with Windows
Basic skills

If you are relatively new to Windows, you have perhaps gone from the first chapter directly to this appendix. Accordingly, we shall give a concise explanation concerning the way in which the keystrokes are described and how the mouse is used. The symbols for the mouse and the keys have already been indicated in chapter 1.

The function keys are referred to as F1, F2 etc. and other special keys as Shift, Alt etc. Pressing several keys simultaneously is indicated by a hyphen between the relevant keys, and keys which are pressed consecutively are separated by a comma.

Examples:
Alt-F4 means holding down the Alt key and pressing F4. Alt, F, X means pressing the Alt key, releasing it, then pressing the F key, releasing it, then pressing the C key and releasing it.

When dealing with the mouse, there are a couple of terms with which you should be acquainted.

Clicking on a word or symbol means positioning the mouse pointer on the relevant word or symbol and pressing the left mouse button once and immediately releasing it. If the right-hand mouse button should be pressed, this is explicitly stated.

Double clicking means exactly the same, only you should press the left mouse button twice in rapid succession.

Dragging means positioning the mouse pointer at a begin point, pressing the left mouse button and holding it down while you move the pointer across the screen to

the required end point where the mouse button is re-
leased.

The windows

As the name indicates, Windows works with windows.
The area on the screen is called the desktop in Windows. When Windows is started up, a window with the
name Program Manager appears:

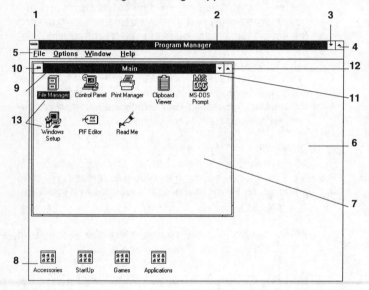

This is actually two windows, one within the other. In the
outer window, the Program Manager, you will observe:

1   *The Control menu button.* This is located in the
    upper left-hand corner of each window. You can
    activate the *Control menu* by clicking on the button
    or by pressing Alt-spacebar. You can use this
    menu to enlarge or reduce the size of the windows,
    to move them or to close them.

2   The *title bar*. The name of the current program or
     document is shown here. If several windows are
     simultaneously active, the colour or shading of the
     title bar indicates which window is active, i.e. the
     window in which you are currently working.

3   The *Minimize* button. By clicking on this, you can
     reduce a window to an icon, a small graphic symbol
     representing the corresponding window. Clicking
     on the icon activates the window again.

4   The *Maximize* button, which allows you to enlarge
     the size of a window to fill the entire screen. If you
     do this, the *Restore* button takes the place of the
     Maximize. Clicking on it will restore the window to
     its original size.

5   The *menu bar*. Under the words in the Menu bar, in
     this case File, Options, Window and Help, there are
     various options available. Under Help, you can al-
     ways find an explanation about the diverse topics
     which you encounter in Windows. In the Program
     Manager window, the Help index provides informa-
     tion about the Keyboard, Basic skills, Commands
     and Procedures, in addition to an index of Windows
     terminology and an outline concerning the Help
     function. Information dealing with the Program
     Manager itself is given under Help. **Window** pro-
     vides options to alter the appearance of a window
     on the screen. **File** enables you to install a new pro-
     gram group (New...), activate a group highlighted at
     the bottom of the screen (Open) or delete it, alter
     the attributes of a group (for instance, assign a new
     name), start up a program or close Windows.

6   The *work area*. This is the area in which other win-
     dows can be placed.

7   The *mouse pointer* (not visible here). Mostly this is
     in the form of an arrow, but sometimes assumes a
     different form according to the situation.

8   Depending on the programs already installed, *icons*
     representing *group windows*: Accessories, StartUp,
     Applications, and Games.

The inner window contains the following elements:

9   The *title bar*. The Program Manager Main Group is
     currently active and therefore this title bar has a
     dark colour (shading).

10   The *Control menu* button in the Main Group. Using
     this, you can change the size of the inner window,
     close the window or reduce it to an icon.

11   The *Minimize* button. This enables you to reduce
     the window to an icon.

12   The *Maximize* button. This enables you to enlarge
     the size of the window.

13   *Icons* representing the programs which make up
     the Program Manager Main Group: File Manager,
     Control Panel, Print Manager, Clipboard Viewer,
     MS-DOS Prompt, Windows Setup, PIF Editor and
     Read Me.

When the Windows desktop resembles the figure
shown at the beginning of this section, you can:

■ make a selection from the menu bar;
■ make a selection from the Control menu;
■ select an application from the Main Group;
■ select another group window in order to choose an
  application.

Making a selection from the Control menu

Activating the Control menu takes place as follows:

M   Click on the Control menu button in the upper left-hand corner.

K   Press Alt-spacebar.

You will obtain the following options:

```
Restore
Move
Size
Minimize
Maximize
Close  Alt+F4
Switch To...Ctrl+Esc
```

The colouring or shading in the menu options indicates which options are available at the moment (those in grey are not available). *Restore* returns the active window to its original size. *Move* allows you to move the window. *Minimum* reduces the window to an icon and *Maximum* enlarges a window to fill the entire screen. We shall return to *Close* shortly. If you wish to select *Switch To...*, proceed as follows:

M   Click on *Switch To...*

K   Type the underlined letter in the menu, in this case, W, or using the cursor keys, move downwards until the required option is highlighted and press Enter. A quicker method of doing this is to press the shortcut key combination Ctrl-Esc.

The three points (ellipsis) behind the option indicate that a dialogue box will be displayed. The following will appear:

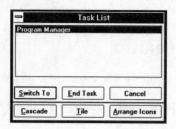

A list of options is shown under the 'Task List' title bar. At the moment, only one option is available, the Program Manager. You can choose from the list of options shown underneath the list. *Switch To* refers to the option in the list which is marked. Since only Program Manager is marked and Program Manager is already active, any choice at the moment will have no effect. The options *Tile* and *Arrange Icons* also seem to have no effect. *Cascade* is only important if several windows are open at once. If you choose this option the Program Manager window will be placed in a corner of the screen. *End Task* leads to the closure of Windows at the moment, since no other tasks are active. *Cancel* allows you to cancel any alterations.

M   Click on the required option to activate it immediately.

K   Use the Cursor Up and Cursor Down keys to make a selection from the list. Using Tab you can select one of the six options. When the required option has been marked (an extra dotted line is shown), press Enter. You can also, when one of the options has been marked (thus, by pressing Tab at least once), select an option by pressing the underlined letter. Do not type a letter to select *Cancel*, press Esc instead.

If you select *Close* in the *Control menu*, a dialogue box will be displayed:

You can then quit Windows by:

𝓂   Clicking on *OK*.

𝓀   Pressing Enter, since *OK* is already marked.

If you do not want to quit Windows:

𝓂   Click on *Cancel*

𝓀   Press Esc or move to *Cancel* using Tab and press Enter.

Making a selection using the menu bar

In order to make a choice from the options given using the menu bar, proceed as follows:

𝓂   Click on the corresponding word in the menu bar. A drop-down list will appear. Click on the required option. If you drag the mouse pointer over the menu bar while holding down the left button, all the drop-down menus will be displayed in succession.

𝓀   Activate the menu bar by pressing Alt or F10. Type the underlined letter in the word you wish to select, and then the underlined letter of the option required.
Or, you can also activate the menu bar Using Alt or F10, mark your choice in the menu bar using the cursor keys (Cursor Left, Cursor Right) and then using Cursor Down or Cursor Up, make a selection from the drop-down menu. Press Enter. When you have pressed Cursor Down once in this situation, you can use Cursor Right

and Cursor Left to examine the other drop-down menus, including the Control menu.

In order to remove the menu from the screen, proceed as follows:

m   Click on a spot outside the menu.

K   Press Alt or F10, or press Esc twice.

Under *Help* in the menu bar, you can find a drop-down menu with a great deal of Help information and the *About Program Manager* option which also allows you to find out how much memory the PC has available and in which mode Windows is running on your computer. If you wish to examine this information, proceed as follows:

m   Click on *Help*, then on *About Program Manager*.

K   Press Alt-H, then I, or
Press Alt, mark *Help* using Cursor Right, move downwards using Cursor Down until *About Program Manager* is marked and then press Enter.
(You may also use F10 instead of Alt.)

The ellipsis behind *About Program Manager* indicates that a dialogue box will be displayed. You can then for example, see that Windows is running in 386 enhanced mode, that 10,884 Kb memory is available and 83% System Resources. The dialogue box disappears if you click on *OK* or press Enter.

Do you wish to know more about a certain topic, for instance icons?

Click on *Help* in the menu bar, then on *Search for Help on...*. A list with topics will be displayed. Specify 'icons' in the appropriate box or scroll through the topics until 'icons' is highlighted. Then click on Go To. The mouse pointer changes into a hand with which you can choose a further topic. If you wish to choose another topic, click on *Back* at the top of this window and make a new choice. When you have found out what you want to know, click on the control button of **this** window and then on *Close*. Or, Click on *File* in the menu bar of this window and then on *Exit*.

𝓣   Press Alt-H, then S. A list of topics will be shown. Move to the appropriate box using the Tab key and then using Cursor Down or Cursor Up, move through the list until the required topic is highlighted. Press Enter. If you wish to select a new topic, type B (Back), make a new selection using Tab and Enter. To leave the window press Alt-F, X.

Do you wish to know more about the Help function?

𝓜   Click on *Help* in the menu bar, then on *How to Use Help*. A window containing text appears, in which not all the text is visible. You can move through the text by clicking on the arrows at the top and bottom of the scroll bar at the right or by dragging the scroll block through the scroll bar. When you have read enough, click on the control button in **this** window and then on *Close*. Or, click on *File* in the menu bar and then on *Exit*.

𝓣   Press Alt-H, H. A window containing text will appear, in which all the text is not visible. You can move through the text by pressing Cursor Up or Cursor Down. To leave the window, press Alt-F, X.

You can return from any Help Window to the Help index by selecting *Back* (Alt-B). You can activate the Help function from any window (except Help) by pressing F1.

Selecting an icon within the Main Group

How do you activate an application in the Main Group?

M   Double click on the corresponding icon.

K   Mark the corresponding icon using the cursor keys. When the proper icon has been marked (this can be recognized by the colouring or shading), press Enter to start up the program.

In the Program Manager window, there are icons representing two or more group windows. How do you open a group window?

M   Double click on the corresponding icon.

K   Mark the icon by pressing Ctrl-Tab as many times as is required. When the proper icon has been marked (this can be recognized by the colouring or the shading), press Enter to open the group.

Imagine, for instance, you wish to play Solitaire:

M   Double click on the Games icon. Double click on the Solitaire icon. In order to close the game: click on the Control button of Solitaire, click on *Close*. Or, click on the Game in the Solitaire menu bar and click on *Exit*.

K   Press Ctrl-Tab until Games is marked. Press Enter. Mark the required game using the cursor keys and press Enter. To finish: press Alt-G, X.

You will still see the Games window on the screen. How do you move to another window?

If you wish to return to Games eventually, you only need to click on the small part of the Main Group menu bar which is still visible, or press Ctrl-Tab. Then the Games window will be placed in the background behind the Main Group.

If you do not wish to use the Games group again in this session, close the window as follows:

m   Click on the Games Control button, Click on *Close*.

K   Press Ctrl-F4.

You will now return to the Main Group window.

Do you wish to use one of the Accessories?

m   Double click on the Accessories icon, or click on Accessories and then on *Maximize* in the list which appears above the icon.
Then double click on the icon of the application which you wish to use.
If you wish to close the application, click on the Control button of the application, then on *Close*.

K   Press Ctrl-Tab until the Accessories icon is marked. Press Enter.
Use the cursor keys to make a selection from the applications and press Enter.
To close an application, press Alt-spacebar, C.

You will then return to the Accessories window. If you do not wish to work with Accessories any more, you can close the window as follows:

m   Click on the Control button, then on *Close*.

K   Press Ctrl-F4.

Exit Windows

If you wish to end working with Windows, choose one of the methods described below. Do not just switch the computer off, this may damage the files used, or a temporary file created by Windows may remain on the hard-disk unintentionally.

M   Click on the Control button in the Program Manager.
         Click on *Close*. The following dialogue box appears:

         Click on *OK* to quit Windows.

K   Press Alt-spacebar, then C. Or Alt-F4. The dialogue box
         shown above appears on the screen. Press Enter to
         quit Windows.

         If you wish to know more about working with the pro-
         grams which are supplied along with Windows, or about
         the way in which Windows settings can be changed and
         new programs installed, it is advisable to acquire a sep-
         arate book about Windows.

Appendix E
Software Indicator

As far as possible, when discussing the software, the most recent versions of the programs are dealt with. Previous versions of some programs are still available. Due to the quantity of software now on the market, this survey cannot possibly hope to be complete.

Word Processing

WordPerfect 5.1 for DOS. In principle, this will run on every PC with a 2.0 version of DOS or higher. At least 640 Kb working memory and a harddisk are recommended. Expanded memory will allow the program to run quicker. Versions in various languages are available, as are language modules (hyphenation, spelling check, thesaurus).

LetterPerfect 1.0. A WordPerfect Corporation product. Runs on every computer with 2.0 version of DOS or higher. A harddisk is not necessary, 512 Kb working memory is sufficient. Files are interchangeable with WordPerfect 5.1.

WordPerfect 5.1 for Windows. Requires a PC/AT with an 80286 processor or higher, a harddisk and a minimum of 2 Mb working memory, running under Windows 3.0 or higher. A mouse and 4 Mb working memory are recommended. The files are interchangeable with WordPerfect 5.1 for DOS files and LetterPerfect 1.0 files. Language modules from WordPerfect 5.1 for DOS are usable in WordPerfect 5.1 for Windows, excepting the hyphenation.

WordPerfect Works. A WordPerfect Corporation product. This is an integrated package including LetterPerfect, a spreadsheet (a limited PlanPerfect version), a database, agenda and communication functions. Not yet available.

Ami Pro for Windows. A Lotus Development product. Has the same system requirements as WordPerfect for Windows. Also has a word processing program with extensive DTP possibilities. Is capable of reading WP 5.1 files and converting Ami files to WP files.

Ami Pro running demo. Working version of Ami Pro, containing word processor, graphics, tables, text formatting, printing and reading in of WP 5.1 files. Spelling check and some other functions not available, edited files cannot be saved. Supplied with run-time version of Windows, thus the demo is usable for those who do not yet have Windows 3.0 or 3.1. Available free from Lotus Development.

Word 2.0 for Windows. Microsoft product. Requires Windows 3.0 or 3.1. Can read and produce WP files. Spelling check in other languages not yet available (version 1.1 does have this).

Spreadsheets

PlanPerfect for DOS. WordPerfect Corporation product. Data can easily be integrated in WordPerfect. The working of the function keys and menus can be as in WordPerfect for DOS or as in Lotus 1-2-3 for DOS.

PlanPerfect for Windows. Files can be interchanged with PlanPerfect for DOS and can be read in the DOS and the Windows versions of WordPerfect.

1-2-3 for Windows. A Lotus Development product. Requires Windows 3.0 or 3.1. Data can be adopted in WordPerfect.

Excel 4.0 for Windows. A Microsoft product. Requires Windows 3.0 or 3.1. Data can be exchanged with other Windows programs.

Graphic programs

DrawPerfect 1.1 for DOS. A WordPerfect Corporation product. DrawPerfect files can easily be adopted in WordPerfect. WP text files can be edited in DrawPerfect (including setting in other fonts and diverse graphic processing).

DrawPerfect for Windows. Easy co-operation with other Windows programs. Resembles WPWin in many respects. Requires Windows 3.0 or 3.1.

Persuasion 2.0. An Aldus product. For presentation requirements, with graphics, text and images.

Arts & Letters Graphics Editor 3.1. A Computer Support product. Provides extensive possibilities to alter the actual letter forms.

Corel Draw 3.0. A Corel Systems product. Requires Windows 3.0 or higher. Suitable for drawing and (de)forming letters. Can import and export files in various formats, including to and from WordPerfect.

Harvard Graphics 3.0. A Software Publishing product. For drawing, graphics and presentation.

Harvard Graphics for Windows. Requires Windows 3.0 or higher.

PC Paintbrush IV and **IV**. ZSoft products. Not to be confused with Windows Paintbrush. A graphics program, creates .PCX files which can be used for illustrations in WordPerfect. Does *not* run under Windows.

Dictionaries and Grammar

Grammatics IV 2.0 for DOS. A Reference Software International product. Various versions: UK English, US English, French, German, Spanish. No special system demands. Smooth co-operation with WordPerfect 5.1

under DOS and can also be used separately. Checks grammar and spelling and provides advice about style.

Grammatics IV for Windows. Requires Windows version 3.0 or higher.

Correct Grammar 3.0. A WordStar International product. Requires 1 Mb harddisk capacity, works under DOS. Grammar and spelling check and style advice.

Correct Grammar for Windows. Requires Windows 3.0 or higher. Grammar and spelling check for texts created in Windows word processors.

The Complete Writer's Toolkit 1.1. Works from DOS. Requires approx. 6 Mb on harddisk. Includes grammar and spelling check, thesaurus and style guide.

PowerEdit 1.0. An Artificial Linguistics Product. Requires EGA or VGA monitor, AT 286 or higher, a minimum of 2 Mb working memory and 12 Mb on the harddisk. Grammar check, style advice, *no spelling check*.

The Writer's Pack 1.0. A Reference Software International product. Spelling and grammar check, thesaurus and style advice.

Dictionaries and Translation

Globalink translation software. Globalink products. Translations programs for English/German, German/English, English/French, French/English, English/Spanish, Spanish/English, English/Russian, Russian/English. Requires DOS 3.0 or higher, 640 Kb working memory and 10 to 12 Mb on harddisk per language combination. A Windows module is available, requiring 2 Mb.

Translate!. A Triangle Software Publishers product. Translation programs include English/Dutch and Dutch/English. Approx. 2 Mb required per dictionary.

Co-operates well with the DOS version of WordPerfect 5.1.

Worddisc. Dictionaries include English/Dutch and Dutch/English. Approx. 4 Mb disk capacity required per dictionary. Co-operates well with the DOS version of WordPerfect 5.1.

Language Assistents. A MicroTac Software product. Runs on any PC. Dictionaries in English/German, English/French, English/Spanish and English/Italian. Can be used as resident in word processors under DOS. Is a language module with limited functionality.

MTX-Reference. A LinguaTech International product. Works with standard and supplementary dictionaries, to which the user can also make additions. Is a DOS program for professional applications. Includes English/German, German/English, English/Dutch, Dutch/English.

Desktop Publishing

Ventura Professional Gold (GEM). A Rank Zerox product. Provides very extensive possibilities for working with lengthy documents (reports, dissertations, books). Can handle WordPerfect documents but not all formatting features in these. GEM supplied.

Venture Professional Gold (Windows 3). This is the Windows version of Ventura. Is a little slower than the GEM version but has all the features of Windows programs. Has the same functionality as the GEM version.

Pagemaker 4.0. An Aldus product. This is the oldest Windows DTP program. Can handle WordPerfect documents but not all formatting features in these.

Publisher for Windows. A Microsoft product. Requires Windows 3.0 or higher. An easily-learned DTP program with less functions than Ventura, Pagemaker and FrameMaker. Can handle WordPerfect 5.1 documents.

FrameMaker. A Frame product. Available for the Unix, Apple Macintosh and Acorn Archimedes systems and for Windows 3. Requires 386 or higher processor, 8 Mb RAM. This is a professional DTP program for manuals, dissertations and other books. Built-in word processing possibilities. Can handle WordPerfect documents, but not most formatting features.

Ami Pro 2.0. Requires Windows 3.0 or higher. Has word processing and DTP features. WP files are adopted with retention of most formatting features. See under 'Word Processing'.

Fonts, PostScript emulation, printer utilities

Type Manager Base Pack. An Adobe for Windows 3 product. Ensures a better display of fonts on the screen. Enables 13 scalable fonts to be printed on almost any printer.

Type Manager Plus Pack. Extension of the Adobe Type Manager, with 22 fonts.

Type Align. Addition to Adobe Type Manager, allowing the form of the letters to be altered.

Facelift for Windows. A Bitstream product. Contains fonts, ensures good screen display and printing possibilities on most common printers.

Intellifont for Windows. Exclusively for Windows 3.0 or 3.1 and the HP Laserjet III printer. Ensures screen display of the fonts in Windows and rapid printing on the HP Laserjet III.

MoreFonts 3.0. A MicroLogic product. Contains 28 scalable fonts and supports both WordPerfect 5.1 for DOS and Windows 3.0 or 3.1. Also supports most common printers.

Typographica. A GST Software Products product with 4 packages of 4 to 8 font families per package. Supports GEM/3, Windows 3 and most common printers.

Freedom of Press 2.2. A Custom Applications product. Is a software type of PostScript interpreter. PostScript files are translated by the computer into graphic files for the selected printer. There is a special Windows version.

Freedom of Press Light 2.5. Slimmed down version of the above program. Runs on any PC with at least 640 Kb working memory and 4 Mb disk capacity. AT/286 or higher is recommended, preferably with expanded memory and/or with a co-processor. Handles Post-Script files with 13 scalable fonts and/or illustrations. An upgrade package with 18 extra fonts is available. Supports most common printers.

GoScript 3.0 A LaserGo product. Requires a PC with DOS 3.0 or higher, 640 Kb working memory and a minimum of 1.5 disk capacity. An AT/286 or higher, expanded memory and/or co-processor are recommended. Can handle PostScript files with 13 scalable fonts and/or illustrations. Extra fonts are available. Supports most common printers.

SuperPrint 2.0. A Zenographics product. Requires Windows 3.0 or 3.1. SuperPrint replaces the Windows Print Manager and provides a large number of scalable fonts. Usable on most printers.

Fonts-on-the-Fly. Provides 19 good, scalable fonts for diverse printers. Can be used in the DOS version and the Windows version of WP 5.1.

TypeMaker. A SoftMaker product. Consists of 4 packages containing various fonts. From version 2.0 onwards can be used under Windows 3.0 or higher but only in combination with the Adobe Type Manager. Is suitable for most printers. Laser printers should have at least 1 Mb internal memory to produce the best results.

Instruction Software

Productivity Pack 1.0 for Windows. A Microsoft product. Instructions on the screen help you get to know Windows.

Shareware and PD software

Public Domain software is available for almost nothing and may be freely copied. Shareware may also be freely copied and tried, but if the user is satisfied and wishes to continue using the program, the manufacturer will expect a (moderate) recompense. If you pay this recompense, you will become a registered user and you will receive a manual and often an improved or more extensive version of the program.

PD software and Shareware provide dozens of utility programs for Windows, in addition to fonts for WordPerfect and for Windows. These programs are available from special suppliers and are sometimes supplied on diskette by various computer magazines.

Appendix F
Terminology

In this appendix, a concise explanation is given for a number of computer, DOS, Windows and WordPerfect terms. Words with an asterisk (*) occur elsewhere in the alphabetical list.

386 enhanced mode: see Enhanced* mode.

Active directory: The directory* which is currently in use.

Active window: Several windows can be open simultaneously. The window* in which you are currently working is the active window. This is indicated by the colour of the title bar*.

Addendum: Addition to a document, in the form of a table of contents or an index.

ANSI character set: A set of 256 characters used by WordPerfect. Established by the American National Standards Institute.

Application: A computer program used for a special objective, for example, word processing, drawing, designing, data management etc.

ASCII characters: The 128 signs which have a fixed ASCII value*. Established according to the American Standard Code for Information Interchange.

ASCII value: The value which a letter, digit or other character has in the ASCII table. This indicates the binary value (a combination of zeros and ones) this sign has in the computer system.

AT: Advanced Technology. A PC with a 80286 or higher processor*.

Attribute: A feature which can be assigned to a file*.

Base memory: see conventional memory*.

Batch file: A list of DOS instructions which are executed automatically in succession.

Bit (BInary digiT): The smallest unit of computer data, consisting of a one or a zero.

Buffer: Part of memory, used to store certain information temporarily.

Button: Graphic symbol for a command to be given or an option chosen. Buttons representing options which are not currently available are shown in a lighter colour.

Button bar: A WordPerfect function which allows you to place buttons in a window yourself so that you can select certain functions or options quicker.

Byte: A piece of information processed by the computer, consisting of 8 bits*. One character (a letter, number or other sign) is represented by one byte.

CGA: Color Graphics Adapter, with a resolution of 320 by 200 pixels*. A CGA card can drive a colour monitor but produces a rather ragged display compared to an EGA* or VGA* card.

Check box: A box in a dialogue box* where a cross can be placed or removed. A cross indicates that the option in question is active. A grey box indicates that the option applies to a section of the selected text.

Click: One quick press on the mouse button.

Clipboard: Temporary storage facility for data from a Windows application. Via the clipboard, data (text or graphic images) can be transferred to another document or another application.

Command button: A button in a dialogue box which implements an instruction by clicking on it. They can also be selected by pressing Tab a number of times. The selected command button has a dark border and a dotted rectangle. The command selected can also be implemented by pressing Enter.

Configuration: The computer setup; which processor, memory capacity, the number and types of diskdrives, the video card etc.

Control menu: A menu which contains commands to open windows* or dialogue boxes*, or to close them, or to enlarge or reduce them. The control menu is displayed by clicking on the control menu button (top left-hand corner) or by pressing Alt-spacebar.

Conventional memory: or basic memory. The sort of internal memory (RAM*) in the computer. Normally 640 Kb is large, XTs and 286/ATs sometimes have 512. WordPerfect for Windows 3.0 requires a PC with 640 Kb conventional memory and at least 1 Mb extended* memory.

Convert: Conversion of a file structure used by a certain computer program to a structure used by a different program. For example, the conversion of a WordPerfect file to a DOS, Word or Ami file, or conversion of a .BMP file to a .PCX file.

Co-processor: An extra processor* which is added in order to allow the computer to execute certain actions quicker. In particular, this concerns processes which demand much calculation. An 8087 co-processor assists an 8086 processor, an 80287 co-processor assists an 80286 processor etc. There is also the special Weitek co-processor.

CUA keyboard: Common User Access. This refers to the way in which the keyboard is used to activate certain functions.

Data communication: Exchange of information *at a distance*. This can be computers in a network, or long range connections using modems and telephone lines.

Data File: A file which is not a program but is created by a program in order to store information.

Database: A collection of data in one or more files, with an established structure, and generally accessible using specially developed programs. Well-known database programs for the PC are dBase III, dBase IV, Foxbase, DataPerfect, Oracle, Paradox, Dataflex, Framework.

DDE links or **OLE links**: A link between files which have been created by different applications (programs) and in which data from one file is automatically adopted in the other file, even when alterations are made. A DDE link is only possible between Windows applications. In addition WordPerfect may be linked to spreadsheets from PlanPerfect, Lotus 1-2-3 and Quattro.

Desktop: The background, behind the windows on the Windows screen. Just as paper or other objects can be moved on a desk, the Windows can also be moved over the desktop in the same way.

Desktop publishing: Editing of text and illustrations using the computer, in order to produce printouts which must fulfil certain quality demands.

Dialogue box: A rectangular frame, mostly for specification of information required by Windows or a Windows application in order to carry out an instruction. A selection between a number of options is often necessary.

Directory: A list or collection of computer files which belong together and which are regarded as a group by the computer. The logical layout of a disk.

Diskdrive: This is normally built-in in the computer. There is a distinction between diskettes* and harddisks*. Diskettes can be replaced, a harddisk cannot be removed from the relevant drive. Nowadays, replaceable harddisk drives are available.

Diskette: A disk with a magnetic layer on which computer data can be placed. The most common types are 3.5" and 5.25". There are *single-sided* and *double-sided* diskettes, and there is a further distinction in the magnetic properties between *single density, double density* and *high density*. The most common diskettes are:
5.25" double-sided, double density (360 Kb),
3.5" double-sided, double density (720 Kb),
5.25" double-sided, high density (1.2 Mb),
3.5" double-sided, high density (1.44 Mb).

Document window: You can open a maximum of 9 document windows in the WordPerfect window. Each window has its own title bar*, menu bar*, and control menu*. If, while working on document, you open another document which is not to be joined to the first one, a new window will be opened.

DOS: Disk Operating System.

DOS text: A text consisting entirely of ASCII characters*, which is stored in a file which can be edited using a DOS text processor such as Edlin or Edit.

Double click: Pressing the mouse* button twice in rapid succession.

Draft mode: A screen setting in which the text can be easily read, but in which the fonts and formatting features are only partially displayed. You can work quicker in this mode since less time is required for the graphical construction of the text.

Dragging: Moving the mouse* while holding down the mouse button.

Drive: see diskdrive.

DTP: see Desktop Publishing.

Editor: Program for processing text files. In DOS this is the Edlin program and, from version 5.0 onwards, Edit. Other editors are supplied with certain PC programs (Program Editor from WP, Notebook from Windows). These programs can only edit ASCII characters, or sometimes only letters (without accents or tildes), numbers and a very limited amount of other characters.

EGA: Enhanced Graphics Adapter, which has a resolution of 640 x 350 pixels. Provides a sharper and more legible display on a colour monitor than CGA*. In practice, the VGA* monitor provides the same quality.

Enhanced mode: The mode* in which Windows 3 runs on a PC with a 80386 processor or higher, with at least 2 Mb* memory (conventional* + extended*). In this way, Windows gains access to virtual* memory and multi-tasking* using non-Windows programs is possible.

Expanded memory: Expansion of the conventional* or basic memory of the PC. Can be added to any PC, and also to most XTs. The size of the expanded memory is unlimited in principle, but is calculated in terms of blocks of 16 Kb. Expanded memory, however, cannot be used to work with WordPerfect for Windows. In the Enhanced* mode, Windows itself can emulate expanded memory for programs requiring this.

Extended memory: Extension of the conventional* or basic memory. In principle, the size of the extended memory is unlimited. ATs with an 80286 processor usually have some extended memory, PCs with an 80386 or 80486 processor always have it. Windows 3 makes use of extended memory if present. In order to run Windows in the standard* mode, 640 Kb conventional* memory is required and at least 256 Kb extended memory. To run Windows in enhanced* mode, at least 2 Mb (conventional + extended) is required and at least a 80386 processor. Windows 3.1 requires 2 Mb or more. WordPerfect for Windows requires a *minimum* of 2 Mb memory (of which at least 1 Mb extended). 4 Mb is preferable. Then you can work on a PC with an 80286 or 80386 processor.

Extension: An appendix of maximum 3 characters (letters and/or numbers) to a file name. The actual name (maximum 8 characters) is followed by a point after which the extension is placed.

File: A collection of data which are gathered in such a way that the computer program can process them and to which a specific name has been allocated. There are program files and documents. Documents may be text files or other data files.

Font: A certain letter style with a certain size and display, for example, Helvetica 12 points bold. All kinds of font features can be specified in WordPerfect, but the printout depends on the printer capabilities.

Footer: Text which is placed at the bottom of the page when the document is printed. This text is mostly the same on each page, although this need not be the case.

Formatting: Preparing a disk (floppy or harddisk) to receive DOS files.

Group: A collection of programs in the Windows Program Manager.

Group window: A window containing programs and data files* which belong together in a group in the Windows Program Manager. An application* program is also linked to the corresponding data files.

Harddisk: A disk made of a hard magnetic substance upon which information can be stored and which cannot be removed from the diskdrive*. Considerably more information can be placed on a harddisk than on a diskette.

Hardware: Devices such as computer, monitor, keyboard*, diskdrives*, diskettes*, mouse*, printer, scanner, modem* etc.

Header: Text which is placed at the top of the page when a document is printed. Generally the same text is placed at the top of each page, but alternative headers are possible.

Hercules adapter: Graphic adapter for running a monochrome* screen. Often CGA* and Hercules are combined on one card. CGA can run a colour screen display, but Hercules provides a higher resolution.

IBM compatible: PC from another manufacturer on which the same programs can be run as on the corresponding IBM PC.

Icon: A symbol representing a Windows group or an application or a function within an application, in the form of a small graphic image on the screen.

Insertion point: The position where text is placed when you type (the current position of the cursor). This point moves continuously to the right as you type.

Interface: The way in which the user interacts and communicates with the computer and the programs.

Kb: Kilobyte, 1024 bytes*.

Keyboard:

LAN: Local Area Network, see Network.

Macro: Short combination of keystrokes which can replace a longer sequence. Can be saved for repeated usage.

Mb: Megabyte, 1 million bytes* or 1000 Kb*.

Menu: A list of instructions appearing on the screen from which the user can make a choice.

Menu bar: A bar at the top of the window*, showing the titles of the menus which are available for that window.

Microprocessor: The heart of the computer. This component, manufactured using micro-electronics ensures that the instructions to the computer are implemented. Most PCs contain an Intel processor with one of the following type numbers (in ascending order regarding age and speed): 8088, 8086, 80286, 80386, 80486. The 80386/SX and 80486/SX are cheaper, slower versions of the 80386 and 80486. Some PCs do not have an Intel processor. They have a comparable processor from another manufacturer, e.g. NEC. An 80286 processor is the minimum requirement for WordPerfect for Windows.

Mode: The way in which applications are run in Windows 3. This depends on the computer setup. There is a distinction between *real**, *standard** and *enhanced** mode. Multitasking* is only really possible in the enhanced mode. In order to run programs which have been developed for Windows versions prior to 3.0, Windows must be run in the *real* mode, using the command **Win/r**. (This is only possible in version 3.0 and not from 3.1 onwards.) WordPerfect for Windows only runs if Windows is started up in the standard or enhanced mode.

Modem: MOdulator/DEModulator. A device which converts the digital signal of the computer to an analogue signal which can be transmitted through the telephone line, and vice versa. A utility in data communication*.

Monochrome: Most common monitors display green, amber or white letters on a black background. Black-and-white screens are also called *paperwhite*.

Mouse: A device which can be connected to the computer and which is used to move quickly to another position on the screen in certain programs. Clicking* is a quick and easy method of selecting an option. There is a distinction between 2-button and 3-button mice. A mouse may be Microsoft Mouse compatible or PC Systems Mouse compatible.

Multitasking: Capable of working with different applications at the same time, in which the working of all these applications continues. In Windows 3, multitasking takes place in enhanced* mode. A PC with at least an 80386 processor and 2 Mb is required.

Network (Local Area Network): A number of computers, joined by cables. Programs and data can be exchanged, usually via a central computer, the *File Server*. Printers can be used collectively. In addition to the individual computer systems (MS-DOS, Apple Macintosh, Unix etc.) there is a network operating system (mostly Novell Netware, sometimes LAN Manager, Banyan Vines, LANtastic) to organize the computer traffic.

Non-active window: A window not currently in use. The title bar* has a lighter colour than the active window. Manoeuvres you make have no influence on the non-active window. A non-active window can be activated by clicking on it.

Non-Windows applications: PC programs which have not been specially developed to run under Windows. These programs can mostly be activated from Windows. They do not make use of Windows special features and generally do not have the same kind of dialogue boxes and menus.

OLE: see DDE.

Option: A selection possibility in a dialogue box*. The selected option determines *how* a command is executed. If a dialogue box contains check boxes*, the various options can be selected independently of each other, more options being possible simultaneously. If a dialogue box contains option buttons*, only one of the options can be chosen.

Options button: In a dialogue box*, there may be a number of options which are mutually exclusive, in other words, only one may be chosen. The option chosen is indicated by the option button.

Options list: A list in a separate box within a dialogue box* providing a list of options from which you can make a choice. If not all options are visible at one time, the list has a scroll bar*.

Parallel port: Connection out, for communication with peripheral devices. Mostly used for printers. Via the parallel port, all bits* of one byte* are transported simultaneously.

Parameter: Supplementary information, or a kind of 'switch' indicating how an application should be activated.

Path and name: The place and name of a file* or group of files or of a directory*. You should specify: the disk name (mostly A;, B:, or C: although this can be omitted if this diskdrive is active), the names of the directories in between beginning at the root* directory, the name of the required directory, and the relevant file.

PC: Personal Computer. The name was first assigned to an IBM computer in 1981.

PIF: Program Information File. A file which informs Windows about the way in which a non-Windows application* should be implemented.

Pixel: Picture element, the smallest graphic unit on the screen. The amount of pixels in a certain area determines the resolution of the graphic display (the sharpness of the image or text).

Point size: The measurement of font size. One computer point corresponds to approx. 0.0012".

Pointer: A symbol in the form of an arrow on the screen. Indicates the current position of the mouse*.

Print queue: The queue of files which are to be printed.

Printer driver: The way in which the printer is operated by an application. In WordPerfect for Windows, it is possible to use either the WordPerfect printer driver or the Windows driver (see chapter 14). The WordPerfect printer driver files can be recognized by the extension .PRS. They are stored in the WPC directory.

Prompt: A sign displayed on the screen, behind which you can enter a command.

RAM (Random Access Memory): The internal memory of the PC. This is in use as long as the computer is switched on. There is a distinction between conventional*, extended* and expanded* memory.

RAM disk: A disk, not physically present, which is made in the computer memory (RAM), quicker and more accessible than a diskette* or harddisk* and more or less recognized by DOS* as being an existing disk. That which is placed on the RAM disk is lost as soon as the power is switched off.

Read only: An attribute* from a DOS file which indicates that the file can only be read but not deleted or modified (overwritten).

Real mode: The mode in which Windows 3.0 runs on a computer with less than 640 Kb* conventional* memory and/or less than 256 extended* memory.

Resident: Program which is loaded in computer memory and which remains present in the background so that it can be activated when required. This is generally a (small) utility program. Loading *superfluous* resident programs leads to unnecessary occupation of computer memory, causing other programs to run slower.

Resolution: see Pixel.

Root: The main directory, i.e. the first directory* on a disk.

Ruler: A function allowing you to set tabs, margins, line spacing, justification and fonts, and to define tables and columns.

Scroll bar: If the contents of a window are not entirely visible, a bar will appear at the bottom or at the right-hand side. This bar contains a small block, the *scroll button* and two arrows, the *scroll arrows*. By moving the block or by clicking* on the arrows, you can draw another part of the window contents into view.

Search path: A specification of the places on a disk where DOS should look for required programs. DOS* first looks in the active directory*, then (if no programs are found with the specified name) in the directories which are specified in the PATH command.

Select: In a document text: indicating the section of text to which a certain command is relevant. Selected text is often referred to as a 'block'. In a dialogue box: indicating that a certain option should be applied in a command given.

Separator: A sign in a DOS text file which indicates the beginning or end of a field or record.

Serial port: Connection out, for communication with peripheral devices. Mice* and modems* are mostly connected to the serial port. Via a serial port, files are transported bit* by bit.

Software: Programs, both the computer operating system (DOS) and programs for word processors, databases*, spreadsheets*, graphic programs, utility programs etc. In contrast to *hardware* (devices).

Source directory: The directory* in which a file is located which is to be moved or copied.

Spreadsheet: A program consisting of a table in which data can be placed in columns and rows. Used particularly for calculation. Spreadsheet programs include PlanPerfect, Lotus 1-2-3, Excel, Quattro Pro, Multiplan.

Standard mode: The mode in which Windows runs on an AT computer with an 80286 processor* and 256 or more extended* memory (in version 3.1 this is 1 Mb or more), or on a computer with an 80836 or higher processor and less than 2 Mb memory (conventional* + extended*). This is only possible on version 3.0; version 3.1 requires at least 2 MB.

Subdirectory: Each directory* other than the root* directory. One or more directories can lie under the root directory, and new subdirectories under these directories. Rather like boxes within boxes.

Target directory: The directory* to which a file is copied or moved.

Text box: A box containing one or more lines within a dialogue box*, in which the user can specify or alter data. This may be the name of a file* or the parameters* in a selected command.

Title bar: Horizontal bar at the top of a window, showing the title of that window.

Variable: A variable unit having a certain name, in which data can be stored for a time. There is a distinction between numeric variables (numbers) and text variables.

VGA: Virtual Graphics Array. Is used to produce a display with a higher resolution* than is possible using Hercules* or EGA* on a monochrome* or colour screen. Some VGA cards can handle different resolutions so that things can be adjusted to the screen available. This screen (paperwhite or colour) must be suitable for VGA.

Virtual memory: Simulated computer memory. Is only available in the enhanced* mode. The total memory capacity consists of the RAM* plus the disk capacity reserved for the Windows exchange file.

Wildcard: A symbol which can replace one or more characters in a file name. ? represents one letter or number, * represents a group of characters (0 or more).

Window: Part of the screen, bordered by a frame, used for a certain application* or file. Windows may be placed underneath, on top or next to each other. A window may also be enlarged to fill the entire screen.

Windows application: Computer program specially made to run in a Windows setup and which cannot be run without Windows.

XT: EXtended Technology. PC with a harddisk* and an 8088 or 8086 processor.

Index